# The Silver Book

**edited by Richard J White**

WOUND MANAGEMENT
WORLDWIDE
A division of ETHICON

Quay
Books

MA Healthcare Ltd

Quay Books Division, MA Healthcare Limited, Jesses Farm, Snow Hill, Dinton, Wiltshire, SP3 5HN

British Library Cataloguing-in-Publication Data
A catalogue record is available for this book

© MA Healthcare Ltd 2003
ISBN 1 85642 253 4

Printed in the UK by Bath Press, Bath

# The Silver Book

# Contents

# List of contributors

Pam Cooper is a Clinical Nurse Specialist — Tissue Viability, Department of Tissue Viability, Aberdeen Royal Infirmary.

Rose A Cooper is Principal Lecturer, Centre for Biomedical Sciences, School of Applied Sciences, University of Wales Institute, Cardiff.

Keith F Cutting is Principal Lecturer, Buckinghamshire Chilterns University College, Chalfont St Giles, Buckinghamshire.

Caroline Dowsett is Nurse Consultant — Tissue Viability, Newham Primary Care Trust, London.

David Gray is Clinical Nurse Specialist — Tissue Viability, Department of Tissue Viability, Aberdeen Royal Infirmary.

Sylvie Hampton is a Tissue Viability Consultant, Eastbourne.

Lorraine Jackson RGN is Clinical Education Manager, Wound Management, Johnson & Johnson Medical, Ascot and is a former Clinical Nurse Specialist Tissue Viability, Leicester General Hospital (now University Hospitals of Leicester NHS Trust).

Kathy Leak is a Sister, Wound Care Services, Doncaster Royal Infirmary.

Liz Scanlon is Nurse Consultant — Tissue Viability, Leeds North West Primary Care Trust, Leeds.

Richard J White is a Clinical Research Consultant and Medical Writer, Cornwall.

# Foreword

Ensuring that our clinical practice is grounded in the best available evidence is an ongoing challenge. Wound healing/treatment is constantly evolving and there is a regular stream of information to be digested. One of the biggest problems we face is that many useful papers are published in different journals at different times relating to a similar subject. This book brings together a series of articles, which originally appeared in Silver Supplements of the *British Journal of Nursing* and the *British Journal of Community Nursing* over a two-year period. Having undergone updating, these papers are brought together to provide the reader with a comprehensive text which both informs and educates. In providing this book the publishers have sought to ensure that information published in different journals at different times are brought together

In the initial chapters the use of different continuums as frameworks for clinical decision-making are presented. These chapters help the reader identify where silver might be most appropriately used within the wound healing/treatment process. Later chapters which review the use of topical agents on wounds, wound microbiology issues and the history of silver in wound healing provide a context against which to judge the current use of silver in wound healing/treatment. The final chapters reflect current thinking and practice with the use of both clinical data and case studies.

Individually, each chapter provides a high standard of information for the reader. Taken as a whole, these chapters provide a book which allows the reader to understand why and where silver has a role in modern wound management.

David Gray
Clinical Nurse Specialist
Department of Tissue Viability
Grampian Health Services
Aberdeen

# 1

# The wound healing continuum

*David Gray, Richard J White, Pam Cooper*

Wound classification systems have been devised in an attempt to provide simple frameworks for non-specialist nurses to assess and manage wounds. However, most have been seen to fail, probably due to over-simplification and failure to validate their usefulness. We have devised a classification system of healing that is based on colour and is an extrapolation of some of those that have gone before. We have taken the time to address the needs of the less experienced carer and have a more inclusive scheme. This is intended to aid identification of the main prognostic feature of the wound, which will serve as an indicator for healing or non-healing and provide the basis for selection of treatment. When used in conjunction with the wound infection continuum, we believe this system will provide an accurate framework sufficient to guide classification and management of most acute and chronic wounds.

Historically, there have been numerous wound classification systems, some broad-based and general, others specific to a particular wound type. None has received universal acclaim and all have been criticized for shortcomings, whether actual or perceived. All, however, have been intended to aid management of the patient — from the simplistic systems intended for basic education, through to the esoteric and highly technical systems intended for the expert.

Some classification systems have depended on a simple colour coding (Cuzzell, 1988; Stotts, 1990; Krasner, 1995; Lorentzen *et al*, 1999). Each of these has relied on a spectrum of colours — red, yellow and black — to equate with granulation, slough and necrosis respectively. By estimating the proportions of each colour present in any given wound, one can use this as an adjunct to traditional classification according to aetiology, dimensions, bacterial contamination and so on. It has been claimed that this colour system helps identify which phase of the healing continuum a wound is in, and, as a consequence, broad guidelines on management. For example, a yellow 'sloughy' wound requires debridement (Krasner, 1995). However, even the author admitted the shortcomings of this generalization by describing two types of yellow wound — the sloughy and the infected/pus-filled. Red can also be too broad a descriptor; granulating, healthy wounds are red as are wounds colonized or infected with haemolytic streptococci. Following a few years of use, the simple, three-colour system has largely fallen into disuse even though a 'moderate' inter-observer correlation has been reported (Lorentzen *et al*, 1999). The three-colour system has been labelled 'an over-simplification' (Hilton and Harding, 2001).

Kingsley (2001) has devised a wound infection continuum. This, too, is a framework for clinical practice. It relies on an understanding of some commonly-used terms and a spectrum which extends from the sterile to the infected wound. This continuum has been further clarified and is the basis of *Chapter 2*.

The wound healing continuum (WHC) that we have devised relies on the identification of the colours present in any given wound and applying the most clinically significant to the spectrum, which extends from black to pink with intermediate gradations (*Figure 1.1*). This system is not intended to replace any of those already extant, rather, it is a supplemental and general system. The overriding principle which dictates the most clinically significant colour is the need to address that component to permit wound healing. So, in a wound that contains any black eschar, the primary requirement is to debride before healing can proceed — without this intervention, there will be no healing. This is illustrated in *Figure 1.2*.

**Figure 1.1: The wound healing continuum**

The development of the WHC does allow the majority of wounds that heal by secondary intention to be included. There will always be exceptions. One of the problems we have with any classification — be it of pressure ulcers or risk assessment etc. — is that people have failed to recognize the anomalies and limitations at the very start.

The two user-friendly continuums discussed in this book can guide clinical decision-making for basic staff, or staff who do not work with wounds on a regular basis.


## The basis of identification

Which colour is of primary importance? As the continuum is followed from left to right, ie. from black to pink, it correlates with healing of the wound. Not all wounds will naturally progress in this fashion. Not all wounds will exhibit black.

In general, it is most important to identify the colour that is furthest to the left of the continuum, then to implement management procedures to eradicate that colour, enabling the wound to progress steadily to the right. Again, generally speaking, each colour or combination will dictate a specific wound management approach. There are exceptions to this rule, but our aim is to use the WHC to support clinical decision making, not to replace it. This chapter does not address the management methodology.

## The black wound

Black has been termed the 'unhealthiest' colour (Stotts, 1990). It is typical of necrosis and has connotations of gangrene and of malignant melanoma. However, black does not always have serious repercussions, as not all black wounds are gangrenous. The fully black wound, covered by dry, hard eschar is illustrated in *Figure 1.2*. This is a typical, benign presentation of the heel pressure ulcer. Where the wound under consideration is a pressure ulcer, it might also be appropriate to refer to a specific classification system at all stages of management (Russell, 2002). Such a classification will include wound characteristics such as depth, and risk factors associated with the individual patient.

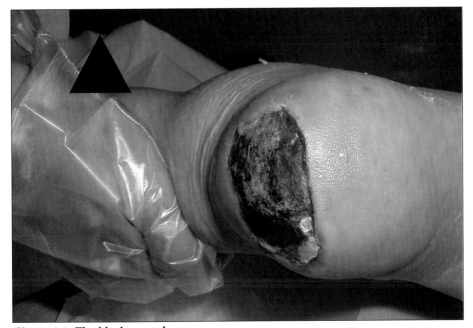

**Figure 1.2: The black wound**

Clearly, in this instance debridement is essential (Torrance, 1983). The method used will be dictated by local policy, formulary and the skills of the individual practitioner. Not all heels will present fully covered with eschar. However, where the ulcer is 'multicoloured' (ie. has red, yellow and other components) then the principle is to classify according to the black. For a wound that has progressed from this early stage, using the same heel wound as an example, the initial debridement of eschar often reveals yellow slough beneath. This then becomes the single most important feature to classify. It dictates that further debridement, possibly by a different approach to that taken previously, is required. It is important to note that the presence of black tissue in a wound is not restricted to pressure ulcers. Acute wounds such as surgical wounds will occasionally develop hard, dry eschar.

## The black-yellow wound

This wound should be classified as a black wound as this is the more 'serious' colour on the continuum. The yellow component usually indicates the presence of fibrous slough, which frequently co-exists with eschar (*Figure 1.3*). A wound presenting with these two colours may be deteriorating to the left of the continuum, or improving as eschar is removed. Consequently, the past history of the progress of the wound, and of the patient's general condition, must be ascertained.

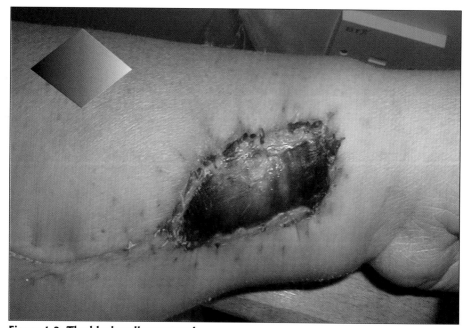

**Figure 1.3: The black-yellow wound**

## The yellow wound

For any wound with a yellow component, first consider the possibility of pus and therefore infection. Once this has been eliminated as a possible reason, then yellow is attributable to slough (Tong, 1999) (*Figure 1.4*). Slough is usually yellow but may also be white; it serves as a medium for the growth of bacteria and must, therefore, be removed (Tong, 1999).

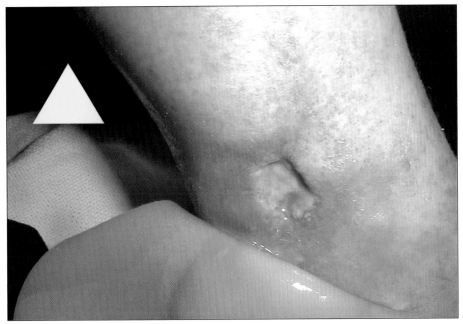

**Figure 1.4: The yellow wound**

## The yellow-red wound

As with all bicoloured or multicoloured wounds (*Figure 1.5*), the wound should be classified according to the most serious colour. In this case the red component is probably due to granulation tissue. However, not all red is positive — some may be attributable to colonization or infection with a haemolytic bacterium such as β-haemolytic *Streptococcus* species (groups A, B, C and G; Schraibman, 1990). These organisms are well-known pathogens in leg ulcers and burns/ plastic surgery. Red may also be attributable to the presence of frank blood, possibly from friable granulation tissue (an infection criterion), or trauma. Once these factors have been eliminated as causes, then granulation tissue remains as the most likely explanation.

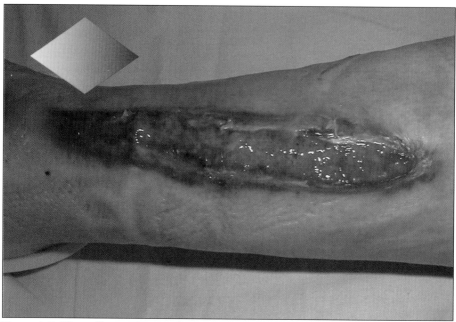

**Figure 1.5: The yellow-red wound**

## The red wound

As stated in the red/yellow section, not all red tissue may be healthy or beneficial to the patient. However, once all other potential causes of the red tissue are excluded, it would be reasonable to assume that the wound is filled with healthy granulation tissue (*Figure 1.6*). It should be remembered that the red tissue may develop unhealthy characteristics such as critical colonization (Kingsley, 2001) and consideration should be given to this fact. Critical colonization of previously healthy granular tissue will result in it failing to heal and possible deterioration in the wound bed.

## The red-pink wound

In *Figure 1.7* the wound can be seen to have virtually covered the granulation tissue with fresh epithelium. At this stage the wound requires a stable, moist environment to ensure the epithelialization process can be completed.

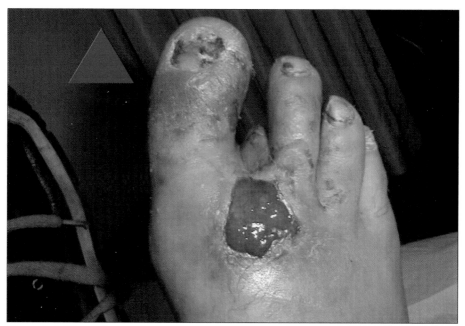

**Figure 1.6: The red wound**

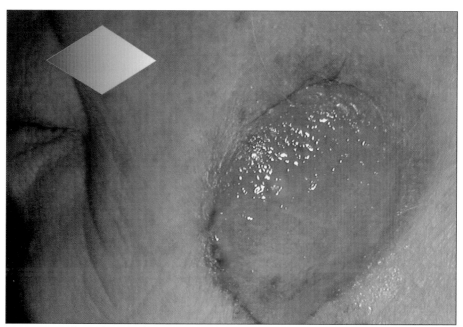

**Figure 1.7: The red-pink wound**

## The pink 'wound'

This is not a wound as such — the pink is due to the growth of new epithelium and so the wound has healed (*Figure 1.8*). It may, however, still require protection until the tissues have consolidated.

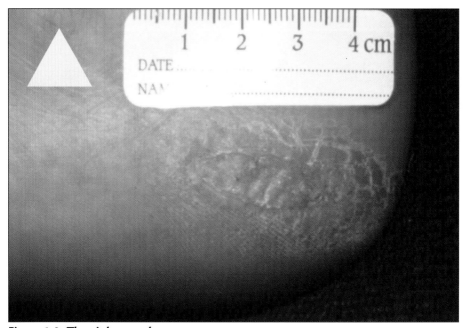

**Figure 1.8: The pink wound**

## Infected wounds

Wounds that are showing signs of green or blue (*Figure 1.9*) are almost certainly colonized or critically colonized with bacteria (Kingsley, 2001). Typically, the bacterium *Pseudomonas aeruginosa* will provide a green/blue colour to the wound (Villavicencio, 1998). In such cases, control of bioburden will be required (White *et al*, 2002). This will be dependant on many factors, eg. the patient's intercurrent illnesses, concomitant medications, risk factors, etc. These wounds are not included within the WHC as they need to be assessed using the wound infection continuum. Using both continuums provides maximum support to the user.

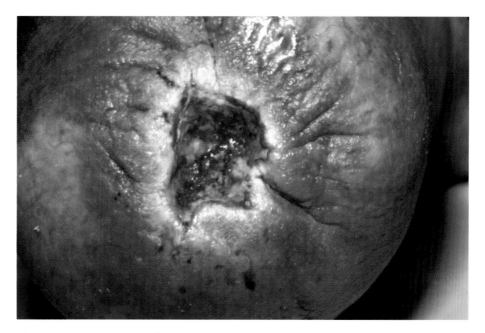

**Figure 1.9: Infected wound**

## Multiple colour wounds

Many wounds will present with a variety of different coloured tissue. As seen in *Figure 1.10* this wound presents with every colour from the WHC. However, by focusing management on the removal of the tissue with the colour closest to the left-hand side of the continuum — in this case black tissue — the wound can be moved along the continuum towards the right/pink end point. As seen in *Figure 1.11*, within seven days the wound has moved to the yellow/red category. In effect, by focusing management on the tissue colour closest to the left hand side of the continuum the wound has in seven days been moved in a positive fashion towards healing.

## Discussion

At present little or nothing is known of healing rates in relation to open wounds healing by secondary intention in the UK. To remedy this lack of information clinical audits are required, which consider the time taken to heal wounds such as pressure ulcers on the heel. Such clinical audits would require a classification tool which would allow for the inclusion of most wounds healing by secondary intention. It is our belief that audits currently under way using the WHC may identify it as a classification tool suitable for such use. Only when baseline audit data is in place will practitioners be able to assess their own healing rates and effectively reflect on their practice. Further work is required to identify the strengths and weaknesses of the WHC. Once such work has been completed, it may be that the WHC and the wound infection continuum will be seen as effective aids to clinical practice in the field of wound healing.

## Conclusions

Within this chapter the authors have sought to introduce a new continuum which can assist in the categorization of most wounds healing by secondary intention. When used in conjunction with the wound infection continuum the user can receive guidance as to the condition of the wound. Both continuums, if used correctly, could also aid long term clinical audit.

## Key points

* ❖ Classification systems are a useful tool in aiding clinical decision making.
* ❖ Existing wound healing classifications have been criticized for being overly simplistic.
* ❖ The wound healing continuum proposed here relies on the identification of the colours present in any given wound and applying the most clinically significant to the spectrum, which extends from black to pink with intermediate gradations.
* ❖ When used in conjunction with the wound infection continuum, the wound healing continuum forms a useful basis for assessment, classification and management of wounds.

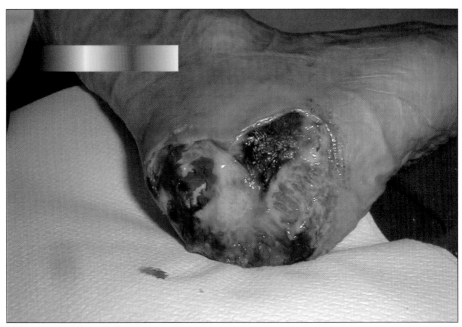

**Figure 1.10: The rainbow wound**

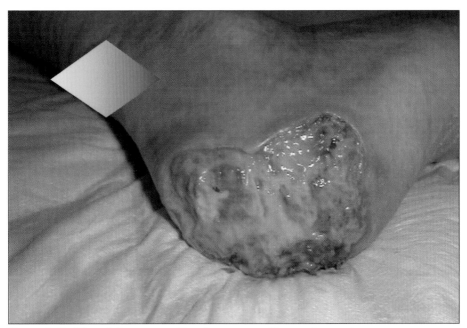

**Figure 1.11: The rainbow wound has become a yellow-red wound**

# References

Cuzzell JZ (1988) The new red, yellow, black color code. *Am J Nurs* **88**(10): 1342–46

Hilton J, Harding KG (2001) Wound bed preparation: a physician's clinical experience. In: Cherry GW, Harding KG, Ryan TJ, eds. *Wound Bed Preparation*. The Royal Society of Medicine Press, London

Kingsley A (2001) A proactive approach to wound infection. *Nurs Stand* **11**(15): 50–8

Krasner D (1995) Wound care: how to use the red-yellow-black system. *Am J Nurs* **95**(5): 44–7

Lorentzen HF, Holstein P, Gottrup F (1999) Interobservatorvariation ved rodt-gult-sort-sarbeskrivelsessystemet. *Ugeskr Laeger* **161**(44): 6045–8

Russell L (2002) Pressure ulcer classification: the systems and the pitfalls. *Br J Nurs* **11**(12 Suppl): 49–59

Schraibman IG (1990) The significance of β-haemolytic streptococci in chronic leg ulcers. *Ann R Coll Surg Engl* **72**: 123–4

Stotts NA (1990) Seeing red and yellow and black. The three-color concept of wound care. *Nursing* **20**(2): 59–61

Tong A (1999) The identification and treatment of slough. *J Wound Care* **8**(7): 338–9

Torrance C (1983) *Pressure Sores. Aetiology, Treatment and Prevention*. Croom Helm, London and Canberra

Villavicencio RT (1998) The history of blue pus. *J Am Coll Surg* **187**(2): 212–16

White RJ (2002) The wound infection continuum. *Br J Nurs* **11**(22 Suppl): 7–9

White RJ, Cooper R, Kingsley A (2002) A topical issue: the use of antibacterials in wound pathogen control. In: White RJ, ed. *Trends in Wound Care*. Quay Books, MA Healthcare Ltd, Salisbury, Wiltshire

# 2

# The wound infection continuum

*Richard J White*

For many people, a wound is either 'infected' or 'not infected'. However, this binary distinction is too simplistic: between these descriptions is a spectrum of microbial involvement. This spectrum has been termed the 'infection continuum', and is a framework for classification, assessment and management of the wound and its microbial load (or bioburden). By recognition of pre-infected stages and appropriate intervention, the progression of a wound to infection could be avoided. Such avoidance would benefit the patient and, by lowering costs, the healthcare system.

Although most wounds heal without difficulty, some will become infected and cause increased morbidity such as pain and loss of function. In some cases, wound infection leads to mortality and, in all cases, increased intensity of healthcare intervention with inpatient stay increases costs. Prevention of infection is therefore desirable.

The transition from acute healing wound to chronic non-healing wound can be avoided by prompt intervention to stop infection (White *et al*, 2001, 2002). This intervention is based on microbiological concepts, knowledge of the normal healing process, and correct interpretation of clinical signs in the wound and the patient.

Heavy microbial load (bioburden) in the wound is probably the most important and common factor in a disordered healing process (Halbert *et al*, 1992; Cooper and Lawrence, 1996a,b; Bowler *et al*, 2001). Delayed healing is the result of disordered cellular cascades stimulated by an unbalanced wound microbe population, causing cellular dysfunction and subsequent biochemical imbalance. Once dysfunction and imbalance are established, they can be resistant to adjustment with commonly used wound-care interventions, as well as being a challenge to more costly emerging therapies, such as protease inhibitors, growth factors and extracellular matrix components (Bowler, 2002). These clinical problems may be addressed by the practice of 'wound bed preparation' and the use of specific protease-modulating treatments (Sibbald *et al*, 2000; Cullen *et al*, 2002; Ghatnekar *et al*, 2002; Vin *et al*, 2002; Veves *et al*, 2002). The presence and implications of microorganisms in the wound have recently been described in terms of a continuum: this provides a framework for the assessment and management of wound bioburden (Dow *et al*, 1999; Kingsley, 2001).

The infection continuum extends from non-contamination through critical colonization to infection. It is best used in conjunction with the wound healing continuum (*Chapter 1;* [Gray *et al*, 2002]).

# Diagnosis of wound infection

## Clinical features

Several signs and symptoms accompany wound infection, but not all wounds will exhibit these at any one time. However, there are 'cardinal' or 'classic' signs that are characteristic in every case: for example, spreading erythema or frank pus. In many cases, the presentation is more complex or subtle. Although erythema around an acute wound in healthy skin, or pus in an otherwise clean wound, would be clearly evident, the same signs in a sloughy leg ulcer with varicose eczema and lipodermatosclerosis would be harder to recognize. To distinguish acute and chronic wounds for the purposes of infection criteria is therefore advisable. The current standard infection criteria are those of Cutting and Harding (1994) (*Table 2.1*). They have been validated by Gardner *et al* (2001), who found increasing pain and wound breakdown to be the most sensitive indicators of wound infection.

| Table 2.1: Criteria for wound infection |
| --- |
| Abscess |
| Cellulitis |
| Discharge |
| Delayed healing |
| Discolouration |
| Friable, bleeding granulation tissue |
| Unexpected pain/tenderness |
| Pocketing/bridging at base of the wound |
| Abnormal smell |
| Wound breakdown |

Source: Cutting and Harding, 1994

Systemic signs of infection, such as raised white cell count (neutrophilia) and raised serum C-reactive protein (CRP) are standard blood measurements for infection. However, for chronic infected wounds such as leg ulcers, raised CRP may not be diagnostic (Goodfield, 1988).

## Microbiological features

During World War I, clinicians recognized that wounds with high microbial loads (or low concentrations of β-haemolytic streptococci) were prone to infection and best healed by secondary intention. The relation between raised microbial numbers and wound infection has been reinforced by several studies (Bornside and Bornside, 1979) and $10^5$ cfu/g or $10^5$ cfu/cm$^2$ became accepted as the thresholds that normally indicate infection when exceeded. ('Cfu' denotes 'colony-forming units', which are single microbial cells or clumps of cells that form distinct colonies when grown *in vitro*: a representation of viable counting in microbiology.) The $10^5$ threshold has been critically examined by Bowler (2003) who concluded that treatment should be based on achieving a host-manageable bioburden rather than relying on a quantitative criterion.

Robson (1997) has discussed the need to maintain a balance in bacterial numbers to promote unimpeded healing. He has concluded that at densities of less than $10^5$ cfu/g, granulation tissue formation proceeds; whereas at higher densities it does not. However, the presence of β-haemolytic streptococci, even at low concentrations, is capable of impeding healing (Schraibman, 1990). Since quantitative analysis is not done in the UK, these criteria are not easily applied.

## 'Diagnosis' or recognition of critical colonization

The quantity and diversity of microbes (bioburden) representing colonization, critical colonization and infection are individual and depend on the quality of immune response of the host to tackle the particular mix of microbes present. They are not, therefore, exact states; nor are they easily definable by microbiological characterization or quantification, but are likely to follow in order from left to right on the continuum (*Figure 2.1*).

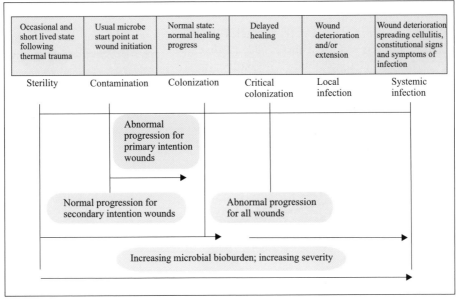

**Figure 2.1: The wound infection continuum (adapted from Kingsley, 2001)**

Some wounds progress quickly from colonization to infection via a clinically indistinct critical colonization state. Such wounds change suddenly and noticeably from normal healing to abnormal deterioration, without ever stopping at a mid-point of 'indolence' or delayed healing. Others will move from colonization to the abnormal critical state and remain there as an indolent, but not visibly deteriorating, wound.

This movement is likely to occur for two reasons (*Figure 2.2*). First, although initially weighted heavily in favour of wound healing due to the host immunocompetency from good health and/or control of underlying diseases, the balance will change in the opposing direction if immunocompetency falls. The existing wound bioburden can now exceed its usual level. The host's controlling immune response can no longer cope with the microbial load. Second, the bioburden increases in quantity or is joined by newly cross-contaminating microbes that increase the virulence of the mixture present, outweighing the immunocompetency on the other end of the scales. When the scales balance, the state of critical colonization exists, and strategies such as the use of antiseptics to reduce the 'weight' (the total number and/or number of species present) of the bioburden will tip the scales back towards healing (Fumal *et al*, 2002). In essence, good wound care adds weight to the right-hand side of the scales. The governing factor in wound infection is the immune response, ie. the host response. Appropriate use of topical antimicrobials can work with the host response to control bioburden and restore healing.

The situation in which the balance is tipped towards infection may coincide either with the expression of virulence factors by the pathogens or with a reduction in the quality of the host response (*Figure 2.2*). There is no evidence to support one factor over the other (Heinzelmann *et al*, 2002).

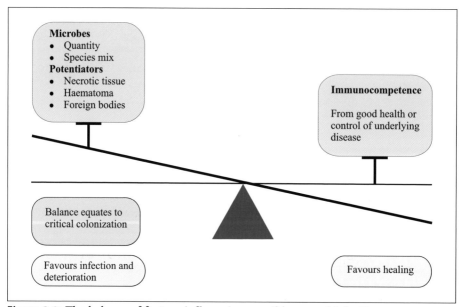

**Figure 2.2: The balance of factors influencing possible wound infection**

This state of critical colonization is most likely to equate biochemically and in cellular terms with the late inflammation phase of the wound healing process.

## Clinical appearance of critical colonization

⌘ Indolent wound, not responding to appropriate care of wound (topical dressings) and underlying pathologies (eg. removal of pressure, reversal of venous hypertension), with no cellulitis.

⌘ Exacerbation of pain, or pain becomes present when it was not before, or change in the quality/experience of pain, still without manifest cellulitis.

⌘ Thick slough not responding to standard techniques (eg. hydrogels, hydro-colloids).

⌘ Fast-returning slough after rapid debridement techniques (eg. larval, sharp/ surgical).

⌘ Intransigent odour.

## Conclusions

The wound-infection continuum is a framework for the assessment of wounds according to microbiological influences. It assists in the identification of key stages of host-pathogen interaction, and so helps in the decision-making leading to antimicrobial therapy. The concept of critical colonization is central to the continuum. It is useful in understanding the role of pathogens in delayed healing and, consequently, can also determine treatment.

When used in conjunction with the healing continuum, this framework for clinical practice can provide the basis for the assessment and classification of most wounds. Further studies are needed to confirm the clinical usefulness of this approach.

## Key points

❖ Diagnosis of infection is based on signs and symptoms in the first instance.

❖ Microbiological investigations can be useful in identifying pathogens and their antimicrobial sensitivity, and in interpreting clinical data.

❖ Awareness of critical colonization is useful in explaining some cases of delayed healing.

❖ When used in conjunction with the wound-healing continuum, the wound infection continuum forms a useful basis for assessment, classification and management of wounds.

❖ Treatment interventions should be based on the need to achieve a host manageable bioburden. Intervention at an early stage, eg. critical colonization, can avoid progression to infection and increased morbidity.

# References

Bornside GH, Bornside BB (1979) Comparison between moist swab and tissue biopsy methods for bacteria in experimental incision wounds. *J Trauma* **19**: 103–5

Bowler PG, Duerden BI, Armstrong DG (2001) Wound microbiology and associated approaches to wound management. *Clin Microbiol Rev* **14**(2): 244–69

Bowler PG (2002) Wound pathophysiology, infection and therapeutic options. *Ann Med* **34**: 419–27

Bowler PG (2003) The $10^5$ bacterial growth guideline: reassessing its clinical relevance in wound healing. *Ostomy, Management* **49**(1): 44–53

Cooper R, Lawrence JC (1996a) Micro-organisms and wounds. *J Wound Care* **5**(5): 233–6

Cooper R, Lawrence JC (1996b) The prevalence of bacteria and implications for infection control. *J Wound Care* **5**(6): 291–5

Cullen B, Smith R, McCulloch E, Silcock D, Morrison L (2002) Mechanism of action of Promogran, a protease modulating matrix, for the treatment of diabetic foot ulcers. *J Wound Repair Regen* **10**(1): 16–25

Cutting KF, Harding KG (1994) Criteria for identifying wound infection. *J Wound Care* **3**(4): 198–201

Dow G, Browne A, Sibbald G (1999) Infection in chronic wounds: Controversies in diagnosis and treatment. *Ostomy, Wound Management* **45**(8): 23–40

Gardner S *et al* (2001) The validity of the clinical signs and symptoms used to identify localised wound infection. *Wound Repair Regen* **9**(3): 178–86

Ghatnekar O, Willis M, Persson U (2002) Cost-effectiveness of treating deep diabetic foot ulcers with Promogran in four European countries. *J Wound Care* **11**(2): 70–4

Goodfield MJ (1988) C-reactive protein levels in venous ulceration: an indication of infection? *J Am Acad Dermatol* **18**(5): 1048–52

Gray D, White RJ, Cooper P (2002) The wound healing continuum. *Br J Nurs* **11**(22 Suppl): 15–19

Fumal I, Braham C, Paquet P, Pierard-Franchimont C, Pierard GE (2002) The beneficial toxicity paradox of antimicrobials in leg ulcer healing impaired by a polymicrobial flora: a proof of concept study. *Dermatology* **204**(Suppl 1): 70–4

Halbert AR, Stacey MC, Rohr JB, Jopp-McKay A (1992) The effect of bacterial colonization on venous ulcer healing. *Aust J Dermatol* **33**: 75–80

Heinzelmann M, Scott M, Lan T (2002) Factors predisposing to bacterial invasion and infection. *Am J Surg* **183**: 179–90

Kingsley A (2001) A proactive approach to wound infection. *Nurs Standard* **15**(30): 50–8

Robson MC (1997) Wound infection: a failure of wound healing caused by an imbalance of bacteria. *Surg Clin North Am* **77**(3): 637–50

Schraibman IG (1990) The significance of β-haemolytic streptococci in chronic leg ulcers. *Ann Roy Coll Surg Eng* **72**: 123–4

Sibbald G, Williamson, D, Orsted HL, Campbell K, Keast D, Krasner D, Sibbald D 2000) Preparing the wound bed — debridement, bacterial balance, and moisture balance. *Ostomy, Wound Management* **46**(11): 14–35

Veves A, Sheehan P, Pham HT (2002) A randomized, controlled trial of Promogran (a collagen/oxidized regenerated cellulose dressing) vs standard treatment in the management of diabetic foot ulcers. *J Arch Surg* **137**(7): 822–7

Vin F, Teot L, Meaume S (2002) The healing properties of Promogran in venous leg ulcers. *J Wound Care* **11**(9): 335–41

White RJ, Cooper RA, Kingsley A (2001) Wound colonization and infection: the role of topical antimicrobials. *Br J Nurs* **10**(9): 563–78

White R, Cooper RA, Kingsley A (2002) A topical issue: the use of antibacterials in wound pathogen control. In: White R, ed. *Trends in Wound Care*. Quay Books, MA Healthcare Ltd, Salisbury, Wiltshire: 16–36

# 3

# A dedicated follower of fashion? Topical medications and wounds

*Keith F Cutting*

This chapter reviews the factors that impinge on the application of topical medications in wound care. The role of systemic and topical antibiotics in wound care is reviewed. Similarly, two antiseptics — iodine and silver, of great current interest in wound management — are scrutinized. The value of these topical agents in the management of wound bioburden should be ascertained from the perspective of understanding the advantages and disadvantages of their use and not established from what is currently the trend.

During the 1980s, the wider use of research in clinical care implied that nurse training had been cast aside and that nurse education was the way forward. This was, in part, a response to the changes underway to prepare nurse education for the twenty-first century (UKCC, 1986).

Nursing pronouncements were sometimes derived from a knowledge base generated by research from clinicians in other disciplines and sometimes this discipline was that of our medical colleagues. This is evidenced by the Brennan and Leaper (1985) article into the effects of antiseptics on a wound model, which helped to seal the fate of Edinburgh University Solution of Lime (EUSOL), which gained pariah status in the wound care arena. Many nurses endorsed these findings, and together with supportive work (Deas *et al*, 1986; Kozol *et al*, 1988) EUSOL was generally confined to the antimicrobial and the desloughing dustbin.

Some nurse writers supported this abolition of a solution that up until then had been one of the mainstays of wound care. Articles were published with emotive titles (Saunders, 1989; Biley, 1991). One enthusiastic supporter, an RCN research officer, even suggested that if a nurse dared use EUSOL then he/she would be guilty of breaking the UKCC *Code of Professional Conduct* (Swaffield, 1990). Cunliffe (1990) took a pragmatic approach at the time and wrote: 'Medical and nursing staff should not be blinded by data derived from experiments which use models that bear no relationship to the clinical situation of a dirty ulcer.'

Today, the way in which EUSOL is applied to wounds varies. It may be left in contact with the wound as a gauze soak primary dressing, or alternatively, it may be used to sluice the tissue which is then flushed with saline. These different approaches will influence the tissue response. That is not to say that one should advocate the application of EUSOL in wound management even if all else fails, but it is possible that selective use may be of benefit in dirty wounds, ie. contaminated with pus, slough and environmental materials. What is clearly evident from published material and the overwhelming feelings of those involved in wound care is that EUSOL has a great potential for harm. Its use is an emotive issue, and at best one of last resort by those with substantial experience in wound care.

## A new fashion trend

Lawrence (1998) has observed the urge to disparage the use of antiseptics when considering topical antimicrobial wound therapy. If topical antimicrobial applications are to be used in practice it is essential for the clinician, if called upon, to satisfy the Bolam principle. This states that actions must be: 'In accordance with the practice accepted as proper by a responsible body of medical men [or nurses] skilled in that particular art' (Ferguson, 1999).

If the Bolam principle was satisfied then a clinician would have demonstrated how he/she has fulfilled a duty of care to the patient (Ferguson, 1999). When making a wound care decision there are two basic considerations: how safe is the treatment, and how effective it is.

Gathering conclusive evidence to support the use, or avoidance, of topical agents is not easily achieved and empirical evidence may have to be used in support. What is important is that those involved in wound care consider all available information and act in accordance with patient needs and local guidelines; inclinations for fashion have no part in this decision-making process.

## Bacterial presence

The skin and mucous membranes play host to a large number of potentially pathogenic microbes. The skin defences, low pH, acidic environment and lysozyme keep these numbers to manageable proportions (Brooks *et al*, 1998). The environment also provides a habitat for a number of pathogens. Any wound, both superficial or deep, is capable of providing an environment that is able to sustain microbial populations, and, if sampled, a variety of bacterial pathogens may well be cultured.

It is useful to note that chronic wounds play host to different populations of bacterial flora to those found in acute wounds (Heggers, 1998; Bowler and Davies, 1999). The equilibrium that exists between bacterial presence and host resistance is a tenuous one. The impairment of the defence mechanisms or an overwhelming number of bacteria will upset this equilibrium and infection may result.

Any breach of the skin causing a wound provides an opportunity for this relatively narrow spectrum of microbial flora to generate an infection (Cooper and Lawrence, 1996). An additional consideration is that non-sterile wounds act as potential reservoirs from which cross-infection may occur (Cooper and Lawrence, 1996).

The perceived bioburden of a wound (ie. the contaminating micro-organisms) may give some indication as to the potential healing rate. In order to assess the risk of infection of surgical wounds, the National Research Council (1964) used the following classification: clean; clean-contaminated; contaminated; and dirty.

Although this provides some guidance to the clinician, a clear understanding of the full implication of wound microbial presence and healing has yet to be achieved. This situation raises a question: at what point do microbes actually influence the wound healing process? Although the concept of a quantitative approach to pathogenic bacterial presence has received widespread support, the actual number of microbes required to generate infection in different wounds remains unclear. This can be anything from $\geq 10^4$ organisms per gram of tissue (Breidenbach and Trager, 1995), to $>10^5$ (Robson *et al*, 1973; Raahave *et al*, 1986), to $<10^6$ (Levine *et al*, 1976). Admittedly, these studies used a variety of sampling techniques on different types of wounds in order to gather the data.

The quantity of bacteria required to generate an infection may also vary with the type of predominant bacteria. Robson and Heggers (1970) stated that the $10^5$ levels of bacteria usually required to generate infection are much lower when beta-haemolytic streptococcus is the offending organism. Alternatively, it is suggested that some bacteria at critical levels of inoculum may provide a stimulus to healing (Tenorio *et al*, 1976; Raju *et al*, 1977). The resulting confusion has prompted the generation of a novel approach, that of the concept of critical colonization (Davis, 1997).

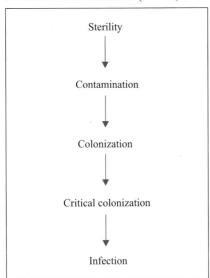

Critical colonization would appear to refer to the point where a wound is unable to maintain a balance between the number of microbes and the defence systems available. This notion of critical colonization has been incorporated into a wound infection continuum extending from sterility to infection (*Figure 3.1*) (Kingsley, 2001). This point in the continuum may help explain the recalcitrant wound that does not show multiple classical signs of infection. For the observer to differentiate between contamination, colonization and critical colonization is nearly impossible as there are no visible cues. The exceptions to this are in cases of pseudomonal or haemolytic streptococcal infection, when the colour of the wound gives indications as to the possible infecting organism.

**Figure 3.1: Wound infection continuum. Source: Kingsley, 2001**

## Antimicrobials

Leaper (1998) reports on a number of issues relating to infection following a consensus meeting of the European Tissue Repair Society and European Wound Management Association. He records that recognition of infection should indicate treatment using an antimicrobial agent. Leaper (1998) goes on to state that the indiscriminate use of broad-spectrum antibiotics raises the problem of resistant organisms emerging and their presence being sustained. This situation is complicated further by the fact that antibiotic choice does not always target organism sensitivity.

However, in the case where clinical infection has been identified, antibiotic prescription may be written based on clinicians' judgment as to the probable sensitivity of the organisms to antibiotics. This indicates the difficulty of managing wound infection, especially from a research-based approach and that often one is left with empiricism (judgment based on experience) as the only guide.

If the point at which microbial presence may influence healing either positively or negatively is difficult to identify, it follows that there is a challenge for the clinician as how best to proceed. At first glance it would seem unreasonable to treat a wound as infected unless it shows signs of classical clinical infection. Although these signs have been discussed widely (Lawrence, 1993; Cutting and Harding, 1994) they are subjective in nature and cannot be considered as organism specific.

## Antibiotics

The problems encountered with antibiotic use and the selection of antibiotic-resistant organisms have been in the public domain for a number of years. Antibiotic resistance is driven by failures of hygiene, overuse, and mobile genetic material that can encode and transfer bacterial resistance. The consequence of this problem has been clearly portrayed as eventually reaching the point where all bacteria could be multi-resistant to all antibiotics. This possibility would take us into the post-antibiotic era (or a return to the pre-antibiotic age) (Brown, 1994). The enforced restriction in use of antibiotics has been shown to decrease expenditure, increase susceptibility of bacterial isolates, and not adversely affect clinical outcomes as measured by survival and discharge from hospital (Woodward *et al*, 1987; White *et al*, 1997).

In a meta-analysis of randomized trials, Cummings and Del Beccaro (1995) could not find any evidence that antibiotics prevent infection in simple wounds. A similar stance is taken by Periti *et al* (1998), who state that prophylactic antibiotics are not recommended for simple, uncomplicated, surgical or traumatic wounds. They do recommend prophylaxis for these wounds if they are heavily contaminated.

Bowler *et al* (2001) support strongly the use of systemic antibiotic therapy when there is spreading infection, eg. cellulitis. Systemic antibiotics should not be employed in wound management unless the wound shows clear features of current infection. Additionally, Bowler *et al* (2001) emphasize the need for all clinical observations, together with microbiological findings, to be carefully considered in the decision-making process. Conversely, Robson *et al* (1974) have shown that systemic antibiotics do not reach the intended target — infected granulation tissue — in chronic wounds at sufficient levels to ensure a therapeutic effect. However, Brantigan *et al* (1996) claim that antibiotics are valuable agents in decreasing the bacterial burden in chronic wounds.

There is the additional issue that systemic antibiotics may promote the colonization of wounds by resistant strains of bacteria (Huovinen *et al*, 1994).

The European Pressure Ulcer Advisory Panel (1999) does not recommend the administration of systemic antibiotics for local infections in pressure ulcers. Also, Bowler *et al* (2001) suggest that this approach may be of relevance to other similar wounds, eg. leg ulcers. Guidelines for the prescription of antibiotics to treat chronic wound infection have yet to be devised (Leaper, 1994).

There is controversy surrounding the application of topical antibiotics in wound management. It is stated that these agents can generate resistant micro-organisms (*British Medical Journal*, 1977) but Leaper (1994) claims that hard evidence for the assertion that they generate a faster spread of resistance is not forthcoming.

A *Drug and Therapeutics Bulletin* (1991) could not support the use of topical antibiotics for routine treatment of colonized or infected wounds on the basis of the lack of evidence to support their use, and the risk of selecting for resistance. There is also the issue of delayed hypersensitivity reactions (Zaki *et al*, 1994).

The advantages of topical antibiotics is that they provide a therapeutic dose to the target area with the avoidance of systemic allergic responses (Bikowski, 1999). They are less likely to affect the commensal population (Bowler *et al*, 2001) and would appear not to be affected by organic matter.

If signs of invasive (spreading) infection are absent, the use of topical antimicrobials may be justified as an initial tactic (Bowler *et al*, 2001). Bowler *et al* also state that if there is no apparent improvement after two weeks then it is doubtful if this approach will resolve the problem and that alternative topical therapy should be considered. If the signs of infection continue, systemic antibiotic therapy may be appropriate.

Mupirocin is an antibiotic ointment effective in the treatment of staphylococcal infections, including methicillin-resistant *Staphylococcus aureus* (MRSA). It is highly unlikely to be toxic to humans (Pappa, 1990). There is mounting evidence available to show that increasing bacterial resistance to mupirocin is occuring (Casewell, 1985; Miller *et al*, 1996).

Fusidic acid is also effective against *Staphylococcus aureus* and MRSA, and both of these agents (mupirocin and fusidic acid) tend to be used to eliminate superficial skin infection or nose/ear carriage. To help avoid contributing to the generation of antibiotic-resistant strains (such as MRSA) some authorities recommended mupirocin for hospital treatment and to reserve fusidic acid for application in the community.

Metronidazole gel is an effective agent against anaerobic infection. An additional advantage is the elimination of wound malodour — a product of protein degradation (Bowler *et al*, 1999).

Neomycin, polymyxin and bacitracin are topical antibiotics that are commonly used in the USA. As a combination therapy they have a broad-spectrum activity, especially against Gram-positive bacteria, but should not be used in pseudomonal infections (Swaim *et al*, 1992).

## Antiseptics

Lawrence (1998) made the observation that 'current fashion denigrates the use of anti-septics'. What instigated this trend is unclear, but the answer possibly lies among a number of factors: over zealous interpretation of research findings; misuse or unrealistic expectations of antiseptics; peer pressure; and locus of control.

Liptak (1997) suggests the components of an ideal wound antiseptic (*Table 3.1*). None of the currently available antiseptics are able to fulfil all of these criteria. However, despite the unavailability of the ideal topical antiseptic they do have the advantage of helping to re-establish the bacterial balance in a wound (Robson, 1999).

The problems of using systemic antibiotics (mentioned previously) prompted a wound care nurse to advocate using antiseptics (Davis, 1996). Using a number of case studies she demonstrated the effectiveness of antiseptics (iodine and silver) when antibiotic therapy fails. Additionally, Davis (1996) makes the important point, for those who are reluctant to use antiseptics: what is more toxic, the cure or the disease?

| Table 3.1: Components of an ideal wound antiseptic |
| --- |
| Effective against likely contaminants and pathogens |
| Fast-acting with prolonged residual activity after a single dose |
| Non-toxic |
| Non-carcinogenic and non-teratogenic to host cells |
| Inexpensive |
| Widely available |
| Incapable of promoting bacterial resistance |
| Minimal systemic absorption |

Source: Liptak, 1997

## Silver

The element silver (chemical symbol Ag), is commonly associated with the white, lustrous metal valued for its decorative beauty and electrical conductivity (*Encyclopaedia Britannica*, 2001). This reference goes on to extol the properties and various uses of silver, but does not include any reference to how silver has been used as a preservative or as a medicine throughout the centuries, or indeed, the application of silver in relation to wound management.

Silver is available in the following compounds: silver metal; silver acetate; silver nitrate; silver protein and silver sulphadiazine (White *et al*, 2001). The advantages and disadvantages of some of these are presented in *Table 3.2*. All of these are antimicrobial in nature (Russell and Hugo, 1994). It is interesting to note that most reports on elemental silver, in relation to infection control or to promote healing, were published before 1940. It is probable that the bad press associated with use of silver relates to the use of silver nitrate solution $AgNO_3$, which may cause staining of the skin (argyria) and a burning sensation on application. Nowadays, there are other vehicles for delivering silver to the wound that do not impart these adverse effects.

**Table 3.2: The clinical advantages and disadvantages of some commonly used silver compounds**

| Agent | Advantages | Disadvantages |
|---|---|---|
| **Silver sulphadiazine (SSD) cream**<br><br>Commonly used as an agent in burn wounds and leg ulcer management | Silver sulphadiazine, silver nitrate and silver-coated dressings found to be effective against a broad range of antibiotic-resistant organisms[1]. Effective against *Pseudomonas aeruginosa* and *Staphylococcus aureus*[4]. Bacteriostatic, painless upon application, soothing effect[3] | May generate a pseudoeschar, promote maceration and retard epithelialization[5]. Reports show microbial resistance to silver sulphadiazine[6,7]. Causes transient, usually not severe, leukopenia[8]. Haemolysis in patients with glucose-6-phosphate deficiency[9]. Risk of kernicterus from sulphonamide component — SSD should not be used during pregnancy, or in infants under two months[10] |
| **Silver nitrate solution (0.5%) $AgNO_3$**<br><br>Ten per cent w/v solution with tannic acid used in treatment of burns in 1934. Proved to be toxic systemically, locally and discarded. Later a 0.5% w/v solution introduced[4]. Soak gauze in warm solution, apply to wound and retain by occlusive or semi-occlusive secondary dressing. This helps prevent gauze drying prematurely and adhering to the wound | Silver is toxic to microbes — it interferes with the cell respiration pathway, electron transport systems and DNA functions[2]. Has wide spectrum of activity, probably more effective against Gram-positives. No known bacterial resistance[11] | Decreased use in recent years due to staining of the skin[12], wound dressings and clothing. Frequent dressing changes of $AgNO_3$ required for it to remain effective. Applications may be slightly painful. Solution does not appear to be effective when eschar is present[13]. When used on large burn wounds electrolyte depletion (sodium, potassium, chloride and calcium ions) has been observed[14]. |

References: 1. Wright *et al* (1998a,b); 2. Cervantes and Silver (1996); 3. Kagan and Smith (2000); 4. Richards and Mahlangu (1981); 5. Klein *et al* (1995); 6. Gayle *et al* (1978); 7. Bridges and Lowbury (1977); 8. Thomson *et al* (1989); 9. Kagan and Smith (2000); 10. Ward and Saffle (1995); 11. Livingstone *et al* (1990); 12. Hill and Pillsbury (1939); 13. Monafo and West (1990); 14. Richards and Mahlangu (1981)

## Silver-containing dressings

There is now a number of silver-containing dressings available. The aim of these dressings is to permit a steady release of small amounts of ionic silver over a period of time, thus removing the need for frequent dressing changes. This sustained release reduces the risk of silver toxicity and helps ensure a decreased bacterial level. A prophylactic and therapeutic mode can therefore be achieved. The toxicity attributed to silver is usually associated with the delivery system, eg. nitrate, sulphadiazine (Demling and DeSanti, 2001) and is therefore not applicable in these dressings.

### Actisorb Silver 220 (formerly Actisorb Plus)

This dressing, manufactured by Johnson & Johnson Medical, contains silver impregnated on to an activated charcoal cloth that is contained within a bonded porous nylon sleeve (Williams, 1994). The charcoal attracts and traps wound bacteria where they are exposed to the antimicrobial effects of the silver. The charcoal also adsorbs wound odour molecules and bacterial endotoxins (Müller *et al*, 2003). In a leg ulcer study using Actisorb Plus, Wunderlich and Orfanos (1991) found that the dressing adsorbed liquid without dehydrating the wound, and that this facilitated cell migration and proliferation. They also found a marked reduction in exudate levels, together with lower bacterial counts than those in the control group.

When comparing Actisorb Plus with silver solutions and a non-medicated charcoal cloth dressing, Furr *et al* (1994) demonstrated antibacterial activity against Gram-negative and Gram-positive bacteria in the silver containing products. Although Furr *et al* (1994) did not find this antibacterial property impaired in the presence of exudate, Bowler *et al* (2001) have questioned the sustained release of antibacterial silver ions from similar dressings when wounds are heavily exuding. However, the dressing would appear to have a broad-spectrum antibacterial activity, including effectiveness against *Staphylococcus aureus* and *Pseudomonas aeruginosa*. Actisorb Silver 220 is available on the UK Drug Tariff.

### Acticoat

This absorbent dressing, manufactured by Smith & Nephew Healthcare, also provides a sustained release of silver but in a nanocrystalline form (Wright *et al*, 1998b). Demling and DeSanti (2001) claim this dressing allows for release of high concentrations of silver when exposed to water, maintains a moist environment and decreases exudate formation through its anti-inflammatory properties. Burrell *et al* (1999) have shown the barrier properties of Acticoat in a wound model study, and Tredget *et al* (1998) have declared the value of this dressing in burn wounds.

Wright *et al* (1998b) claim that Acticoat was found to have a higher silver content than Arglaes, a film dressing, *in vitro*, and that this should maintain bioactivity over a longer period of time in comparison with Arglaes. They also claim that Acticoat does not impair *in vivo* wound healing. Currently, Acticoat is not on the UK Drug Tariff.

## Arglaes

Williams (1997) states that this film dressing, manufactured by Maersk Medical, provides a continuous release of silver ions and has been developed in response to the emergence of resistant organisms resulting from topical antibiotic misuse. This dressing uses silver salts incorporated into a complex of calcium and sodium phosphates (Wright *et al*, 1998b). The silver is released as it comes in contact with wound fluid. Arglaes has been shown to inhibit the growth bacteria with a superior performance against Gram-negative bacteria in comparison with Gram-positive bacteria or fungi (Wright *et al*, 1998a).

## Iodine

Gulliver (1999) illustrates the continuing controversy over the use of this antiseptic. Concerns have probably been generated from toxicity reports that generally refer to older preparations such as tinctures and solutions of higher concentrations of iodine (Gilchrist, 1997). The deleterious effects attributed to iodine from *in vitro* and *in vivo* studies generally do not discriminate between the iodine and its carrier agent, neither do they take into account the rate of delivery to the wound which effects iodine's toxicity (Mertz *et al*, 1999).

Goldenheim (1993) describes why the polyvinyl pyrrolidone iodine PVP-I and delayed wound healing issue is difficult to address. He cites some investigators who have incorrectly applied adverse findings from one preparation to all PVP-I preparations and how others have used questionable wound healing models, ie. data gathered from *in vitro* models may not be pertinent to the *in vivo* situation.

Nowadays, PVP-I formulations are regarded as safe and have been referred to as 'tamed iodine' (Zamora, 1986). They are successful bactericidal agents, including effectiveness against MRSA (Mertz *et al*, 1999). The use of Inadine is not precluded in those whose thyroid disease or diabetes mellitus is controlled by medication. The advantages and disadvantages of the modern iodine dressing formulation are presented in *Table 3.3*.

Iodine is also available as a spray powder (Savlon Dry 1.14%, manufactured by Novartis), and Povidone-Iodine dry powder spray 2.5% (manufactured by SSL International). White *et al* (2001) suggest a role for recommended topical anti-microbials (silver and iodine) in critically colonized and infected wounds (*Figure 3.2*).

There are a number of areas in the topical medications debate that require further answers, and recent developments indicate that confidence in modern preparations of silver and iodine may offer a safe and effective approach to wound care. With the ongoing problem of microbial resistance to antibiotics, antiseptics may have a role in managing infection (Cooper, 1996). Although there is a paucity of *in vivo* evidence to support the use of silver and iodine products, their potential seems to lie in being effective antibacterial wound agents (White *et al*, 2001). In 1915, Bowlby (cited by Davis, 1996) announced the benefits of antiseptics when he said:

> *We did use antiseptics and the wounds described have done consistently better than those of previous years.*

We need to move on from this empirical position and embark on a programme of *in vivo* clinical trials that demonstrate the true value these agents are capable of maintaining in wound care today.

| Table 3.3: The advantages and disadvantages of modern iodine dressings in wound management | | |
|---|---|---|
| **Agent** | **Effects** | **Disadvantages** |
| **Polyvinyl pyrrolidone iodine (PVP-1)** <br> Available in a variety of forms | Effective therapy for topical application with burns victims[1]. Iodine is effective against bacteria, their spores, fungi, protozoa and viruses[2]. Non-staining[9]. Bactericide, sporicide[10] | May cause local irritation/contact dermatitis[3]. Metabolic acidosis may occur with extended exposure[4]. Inactivated by wound exudate[5]. Eschar forms under PVP-I on burns[11]. Should not be used on burns if >20% of body surface[12]. PVP-I not to be used during pregnancy, with the newborn or small children, nor those suffering from thyroid disease[1] |
| **Betadine** <br> **7.5% PVP-I** | Broad-spectrum preoperative skin preparation/surgical scrub | Causes irritation on wound application due to detergent base |
| **Inadine** <br> Rayon dressing incorporating 10% povidone iodine | Prophylaxis and treatment of infection in a wide range of wounds. Skin irritation is rare. Effective against MRSA. Non-adherent. Under medical supervision no stipulated limit to duration of use. More than one layer at a time can be applied to give long-acting slow-release effect. Can be used in shallow cavities | Not ideal for bleeding or highly exuding wounds. Not to be used on pregnant or lactating women and children under two years of age |
| **Cadexomer iodine** <br> Iodosorb — ointment or powder <br> Iodoflex — dressing | Stimulates granulation, reduces erythema, debrides[6]. Safe, effective, economic, high absorptive capacity[8]. Effective against *Staphylococcus aureus*, ß-haemolytic streptococci, pseudomonads[6,14]. Effective in dirty, odorous leg ulcers. Iodoflex changes colour — dark brown to off-white — when iodine has been released. Iodoflex is biodegradeable | Pain during use[7] |

References: 1. Steen (1993); 2. Lawrence (1998); 3. Tosti *et al* (1990); 4. Dela Cruz *et al* (1987): 5. Monafo and West (1990); 6. Skog *et al* (1983); 7. Hansson (1998); 8. Sundberg and Meller (1997); 9. Higgins (1975); 10. Gershenfeld (1962); 11. Steen (1993); 12. Meakins and Pietsch (1976); 13. Steele *et al* (1986); 14. Danielsen *et al* (1997); Steen (1993); MRSA = methicillin-resistant *Staphylococcus aureus*

| |
|---|
| Increasing bacterial resistance to antibiotics and evidence against topical antibiotics |
| Infection control by alternative means |
| Silver and iodine are potent antimicrobials with broad spectrum and little resistance |
| Silver or iodine in a sustained slow-release delivery system for application to wounds |
| Steady release of antimicrobial over a period of days or until removal of dressing |
| Continuous antimicrobial effect |

**Figure 3.2: Thought and decision-making pathway in the use of topical silver and iodine wound care**

## Key points

❖ Antibiotics are not recommended for local wound infection or for simple wound prophylaxis.

❖ Systemic antibiotics should be prescribed for advancing chronic wound infection.

❖ With a few exceptions (mupirocin, metronidazole) topical antibiotics are not recommended.

❖ Iodine and silver in their contemporary formats appear to be of clinical benefit in prophylactic and treatment modes.

## References

Biley F (1991) There will be no euology. *Nursing* **4**(37): 21–2

Bikowski J (1999) Secondarily infected wounds and dermatoses: a diagnosis and treatment guide. *J Emerg Surg* **17**: 197–206

Bowler PG, Davies BJ (1999) The microbiology of acute and chronic wounds. *Wounds* **11**(4): 72–8

Bowler PG, Davies BJ, Jones SA (1999) Microbial involvement in chronic wound malodour. *J Wound Care* **8**(5): 216–18

Bowler PG, Duerden BI, Armstrong DG (2001) Wound microbiology and associated approaches to wound management. *Clin Microbiol Rev* **14**(2): 244–69

Brantigan CO, Senkowsky FJ, Yim D (1996) The effect of systemic antibiotics on the bacterial flora of chronic wounds. *Wounds* **8**(4): 118–24

Brennan SS, Leaper DJ (1985) The effects of antiseptics on the healing wound: a study using the rabbit ear chamber. *Br J Surg* **72**: 780–2

Breidenbach WC, Treager S (1995) Quantitative culture technique and infection in complex wounds of the extremities closed with free flaps. *Plast Reconstr Surg* **95**: 860–5

Bridges K, Lowbury EJL (1977) Drug resistance in relation to the use of silver sulphadiazine cream in a burns unit. *J Clin Pathol* **30**: 160–4

British Medical Journal (1977) Topical antibiotics (editorial). *Br Med J* **1**: 494

Brooks GF, Butel JS, Morse SA (1998) *Jawetz, Melnick and Adelberg's Medical Microbiology*. Appleton and Lange, Stamford, Connecticut: 178

Brown N (1994) Dawn of the post-antibiotic age? *Br Med J* **309**: 615

Burrell R, Heggers J, Wright J (1999) Efficacy of silver coated dressings in a burn sepsis model. *Wounds* **11**: 64–71

Casewell MW (1985) New threats to the control of methicillin-resistant *Staphylococcus aureus*. *J Hosp Infect* **30**: 465–71

Cervantes C, Silver S (1996) Metal resistance in Pseudomonas: genes and mechanisms. In: Nakazawa T, Furukawa K, Haas D, Silver S, eds. *Molecular Biology of Pseudomonads*. Washington American Society for Microbiology, Washington DC

Cooper R (1996) The role of antimicrobial agents in wound care. *J Wound Care* **5**(8): 374–80

Cooper R, Lawrence JC (1996) The prevalence of bacteria and implications for infection control. *J Wound Care* **5**(6): 291–5

Cummings P, Del Beccaro MA (1995) Antibiotics to prevent infection of simple wounds: a meta-analysis of randomized studies. *Am J Emerg Med* **13**: 396–400

Cunliffe WJ (1990) EUSOL — to use or not to use? *Dermatology in Practice* April/May: 5–7

Cutting KF, Harding KG (1994) Criteria for identifying wound infection. *J Wound Care* **3**(4): 198–201

Danielsen L, Cherry GW, Harding K *et al* (1997) Cadexomer-iodine in ulcers colonized by *Pseudomonas aeruginosa*. *J Wound Care* **6**(4):169–72

Davis E (1996) *Do Not Deny the Chance to Heal*. Poster presentation. 2nd Joint Meeting of the Wound Healing Society and the European Tissue Repair Society, Boston

Davis E (1997) *Microbiology Reports and the Chronic Wound. A Nurse's Perspective*. Poster Presentation, European Wound Management Association Conference, Milan

Deas J, Billings P, Brennan S, Silver I, Leaper D (1986) The toxicity of commonly used antiseptics on fibroblasts in tissue culture. *Phlebology* **1**: 205–9

Dela Cruz F, Brown DH, Leikien JB *et al* (1987) Iodine absorption after topical administration. *Western J Med* **146**: 43–5

Demling RH, DeSanti L (2001) The role of silver in wound healing. Part 1: effects of silver on wound management. *Wounds* **13** (Supplement 1): A3–A15

Drug and Therapeutics Bulletin (1991) Local applications to wounds 1: cleansers, antibacterials, debriders. *Drug and Therapeutics Bulletin* **29**(24): 93–5

Encyclopaedia Britannica (2001) http://www.britannica.com/ (accessed June 2001)

European Pressure Ulcer Advisory Panel (1999) *Guidelines on treatment of pressure ulcers*. EPUAP Review 1: 31–3

Ferguson AL (1999) Legal implications of clinical governance. In: Lugon M, Secker-Walker J, eds. *Clinical Governance. Making it Happen*. Royal Society of Medicine Press, London

Furr JR, Russell AD, Turner TD *et al* (1994) Antibacterial activity of Actisorb Plus, Actisorb and silver nitrate. *J Hosp Infect* **27**(3): 201–8

Gayle WE, Mayhall CG, Lamb VA *et al* (1978) Resistant enterobacter cloacae in a burn centre. The ineffectiveness of silver sulphadiazine. *J Trauma* **18**: 317–23

Gershenfeld L (1962) Povidone-iodine as a sporicide. *Am J Pharmacol* **134**: 78–81

Gilchrist B (1997) Should iodine be reconsidered in wound management? *J Wound Care* **6**(3): 148–50

Goldenheim PD (1993) An appraisal of povidone-iodine and wound healing. *Postgrad Med J* **69**: S3, S97–S105

Gulliver G (1999) Arguments over iodine. *Nurs Times* **95**(27): 68–70

Hansson C (1998) The effects of cadexomer iodine paste in the treatment of venous leg ulcers compared with hydrocolloid dressing and paraffin gauze dressing. Cadexomer Iodine Study Group. *Int J Dermatol* **37**(5): 390–6

Heggers JP (1998) Defining infection in chronic wounds: does it matter? *J Wound Care* **7**(8): 389–92

Higgins DG (1975) Povidone iodine: the tamed iodine. *Chemist and Druggist* August 30: 274–5

Hill WR, Pillsbury DM (1939) *Argyria: The Pharmacology of Silver*. Baillière Tindall, London

Huovinen S, Kotilainen P, Jarvinen H *et al* (1994) Comparison of ciprofloxacin or trimethoprim therapy for venous leg ulcers: results of a pilot study. *J Am Acad Dermatol* **31**(2): 279–81

Kagan R, Smith SC (2000) Evaluation and treatment of thermal injuries. *Dermatol Nurs* **12**(5): 334–50

Klein DG, Fritsch DE, Amin SG (1995) Wound infection following trauma and burn injuries. *Crit Care Nurs Clin N Am* **7**: 627–42

Kingsley A (2001) A proactive approach to wound infection. *Nurs Standard* **15**(30): 50–8

Kozol RA, Gillies C, Elgebaly SA (1988) Effects on sodium hypochlorite (Dakin's solution) on cells of the wound module. *Arch Surg* **123**: 420–3

Lawrence JC (1993) Wound infection. *J Wound Care* **2**(5): 277–80

Lawrence JC (1998) The use of iodine as an antiseptic agent. *J Wound Care* **7**(8): 421–5

Leaper DJ (1994) Prophylactic and therapeutic role of antibiotics in wound care. *Am J Surg* **167**(1a Suppl): S15–S20

Leaper (1998) Defining infection. *J Wound Care* **7**(8): 373

Levine NS, Lindberg RB, Mason AD, Pruitt BA (1976) The quantitative wound culture and smear: a quick simple method for determining the number of viable bacteria on open wounds. *J Trauma* **16**: 89–4

Liptak JM (1997) An overview of the topical management of wounds. *Austral Vet J* **75**(6): 408–13

Livingstone DH, Cryer HG, Miller FB *et al* (1990) A randomized prospective study of topical agents on skin grafts after thermal injury. *Plast Reconstr Surg* **86**: 1059–64

Meakins JL, Pietsch JB (1976) Povidone-iodine toxicity. *Lancet* **ii**: 207

Mertz PM, Oliviera-Gandia MF, Davis S (1999) The evaluation of a cadexomer iodine wound dressing on methicillin-resistant *Staphylococcus aureus* (MRSA) in acute wounds. *Dermatol Surg* **25**(2): 89–93

Miller MA, Dascal A, Portnoy J, Mendelson J (1996) Development of mupirocin resistance among methicillin-resistant *Staphylococcus aureus* after widespread use of nasal mupirocin ointment. *J Infect Contr Hosp Epidemiol* **17**(12): 811–13

Monafo WW, West MA (1990) Current treatment recommendations for topical burn therapy. *Drugs* **40**: 364–73

Müller G, Winkler Y, Kramer A (2003) Antibacterial activity and endotoxin-binding capacity of Actisorb Silver 220. *J Hosp Infect* **53**(3): 211–14

National Research Council (1964) National Academy of Sciences National Research Council, Division of Medical Sciences, Ad Hoc Committee of the Committee on Trauma. *Ann Surg* **160**(Supplement 2): 1

Pappa KA (1990) The clinical development of mupirocin. *J Am Acad Dermatol* **22**: 873–9

Periti T, Tonelli F, Mini E (1998) Selecting antibacterial agents for the control of surgical infection. *J Chemotherapy* **10**: 83–90

Raahave D, Friis-Moller A, Bjerre-Jepson K *et al* (1986) The infective dose of aerobic and anaerobic bacteria in postoperative wound sepsis. *Arch Surg* **121**: 924–9

Raju DR, Jindrak K, Weiner M, Enquist IF (1977) A study of the critical bacterial inoculum to cause a stimulus to wound healing. *Surg Gynaecol Obstet* **144**: 347–50

Richards RME, Mahlangu GN (1981) Therapy for burn wound infection. *J Clin Hosp Pharm* **6**: 233–43

Robson MC (1999) Lessons gleaned from the sport of wound watching. *Wound Repair Regen* **7**(1): 2–6

Robson MC, Heggers JP (1970) Delayed wound closures based on bacterial counts. *J Surg Oncol* **2**: 379–83

Robson MC, Krizek TJ, Heggers JP (1973) Biology of surgical infection. In: Ravitch MM, ed. *Current Problems in Surgery*. Year Book Medical, Chicago

Robson MC, Edstrom LE, Krizek TJ, Groskin MG (1974) The efficacy of systemic antibiotics in the treatment of granulating wounds. *J Surg Res* **16**: 229–306

Russell AD, Hugo WB (1994) Antimicrobial activity and action of silver. In: Ellis GP, Luscombe DK, eds. *Progress in Medicinal Chemistry*. Vol 31. Elsevier Science BV, Amsterdam: 354

Saunders J (1989) Toilet cleaner for wound care? *Community Outlook* March: 11–13

Skog E, Arnesjo B, Troeng T *et al* (1983) A randomized trial comparing cadexomer iodine and standard treatment in the outpatient management of chronic venous ulcers. *Br J Dermatol* **109**: 77–83

Steele K, Irwin G, Dowds N (1986) Cadexomer iodine in the management of venous leg ulcers in general practice. *The Practitioner* **230**(1411): 63–8

Steen M (1993) Review of the use of povidone-iodine (PVP-I) in the treatment of burns. *Postgrad Med J* **69**(Suppl 3): S84–S9

Sundberg J, Meller R (1997) A retrospective review of the use of cadexomer iodine in the treatment of wounds. *Wounds* **9**(3): 68–6

Swaffield L (1990) Quest for quality. *Nurs Times* **86**(12): 16–17

Swaim SF, Riddell KP, McGuire JA (1992) Effects of topical medications on the healing of open pad wounds in dogs. *J Am Animal Hospital Assoc* **28**: 499–502

Tenorio A, Jindrak K, Weiner M *et al* (1976) Accelerated healing in infected wounds. *Surg Gynaecol Obstet* **142**: 537–43

Thomson PD, Moore NP, Rice TL, Prasad JK (1989) Leukopenia in acute thermal injury: evidence against topical silver sulfadiazine as the causative agent. *J Burn Care Rehabil* **10**: 418–20

Tosti A, Vincenzi C, Bardazzi F, Mariani R (1990) Allergic contact dermatitis due to povidone-iodine. *Contact Dermatitis* **23**(3): 197–8

Tredget EE, Shankowsky HA, Groenveld A, Burrell R (1998) A matched-pair, randomized study evaluating the efficacy and safety of Acticoat silver-coated dressing for the treatment of burn wounds. *J Burn Care Rehabil* **19**: 531–7

United Kingdom Central Council for Nursing, Midwifery and Health Visiting (1986) *Project 2000: A New Perspective for Practice*. UKCC, London

Ward RS, Saffle JR (1995) Topical agents in burn and wound care. *Phys Ther* **75**(6): 525–38

White AC, Atmar RL, Wilson J, Cate TR, Stager CE, Greenberg SB (1997) Effects of requiring prior authorization for selected antimicrobials: expenditure, susceptibilities and clinical outcomes. *Clin Infect Dis* **25**: 230–9

White R, Cooper R, Kingsley A (2001) Wound colonization and infection: the role of topical antimicrobials and guidelines in management. *Br J Nurs* **10**(9): 563–78

Woodward RS, Medoff G, Smith MD, Gray JL (1987) Antibiotic cost savings from formulary restrictions and physician monitoring in a medical-school-affiliated hospital. *Am J Med* **83**: 817–23

Wright JB, Hansen DL, Burrell RE (1998a) The comparative efficacy of two antimicrobial barrier dressings. *In vitro* examination of two controlled release silver dressings. *Wounds* **10**(6): 179–88

Wright JB, Lam K, Burrell RE (1998b) Wound management in an era of increasing bacterial antibiotic resistance: a role for topical silver treatment. *Am J Infect Contr* **26**(6): 572–7

Williams C (1994) Actisorb Plus in the treatment of exuding infected wounds. *Br J Nurs* **3**(15): 786–8

Wunderlich U, Orfanos CE (1991) Treatment of venous ulcera cruris with dry wound dressings. Phase overlapping use of silver impregnated activated charcoal xerodressing [In German]. *Hautarzt* **42**(7): 446–50

Zaki I, Shall L, Dalziel KL (1994) Bacitracin: a significant sensitiser in leg ulcer patients? *Contact Dermatitis* **31**: 92–4

Zamora JL (1986) Chemical and microbiologic characteristics and toxicity of povidone-iodine solutions. *Am J Surg* **151**: 400–6

# 4

# Wound microbiology: past, present and future

*Rose A Cooper*

Investigations into the causes of wound infection began in the late nineteenth century. In modern diagnostic laboratories the isolation, cultivation and identification of wound pathogens is still important, but routine sampling and recovery methods have limitations. Molecular techniques for characterizing species in clinical specimens may revolutionize our knowledge and understanding of microbial communities in wounds.

Although observations of microorganisms were first made in the seventeenth century with light microscopes, it was not until the nineteenth century that techniques for their isolation and cultivation in the laboratory were developed, and their properties investigated. The nature of contagion had interested investigators for many generations, but the involvement of microorganisms in infectious disease was not clearly recognized until the formulation of the 'germ theory' of disease by Robert Koch in 1876, when the causative agent of anthrax was deduced. In 1884, Koch formulated a set of criteria that came to be known as Koch's postulates (*Table 4.1*). Compliance with these postulates helped to establish the role of many other pathogens in infectious diseases, including wound infections. In 1874, Billroth observed streptococci in wounds (Jones, 1978); in 1878, Koch observed staphylococci in pus. In 1880, Pasteur cultivated staphylococci in pure culture in the laboratory; in 1881, a Scottish surgeon, Sir Alexander Ogston, associated them with acute and chronic abscesses. In France, in 1882, Carl Gessard isolated *Bacillus pyocyaneus* from two patients with bluish-green pus in superficial wounds (Villavicencio, 1998). This Gram-negative bacterium came to be known as the blue pus organism because of its blue-green water-soluble pigment (pyocyanin), but it was later re-named *Pseudomonas aeruginosa*. Shortly afterwards, clostridia were implicated in wound infection when Rosenbach identified *Clostridium tetani* in cases of human tetanus in 1886 — even though the organisms were not cultivated in pure cultures until 1889 by Kitasato (Willis, 1969). By the late nineteenth century, the four major types of wound pathogens had been recognized, and approaches to modern diagnostic microbiology had been shaped. Today,

| Table 4.1: Koch's postulates | |
|---|---|
| 1 | The potential pathogen must be absent from healthy individuals, but present in all cases of the disease |
| 2 | The organism must be isolated from diseased individuals and cultivated in pure culture in the laboratory |
| 3 | Inoculation of pure cultures of the isolate into healthy susceptible animals must cause the disease to occur |
| 4 | The organism must be re-isolated from the diseased experimental case and be seen to be similar to the original isolate |

routine investigations into wound pathogens still attempt to isolate, cultivate and identify pure cultures.

## Routine microbiological investigation of wounds

Most open wounds support polymicrobial communities (Bowler *et al*, 2001), but differences have been found in those species recovered from acute and chronic wounds (Bowler and Davies, 1999a) and from infected and non-infected wounds (Bowler and Davies, 1999b). When wound healing proceeds normally, routine microbial investigation is not appropriate: it is indicated only when a clinical judgement is uncertain or an empirical antimicrobial intervention has failed and an alternative agent must be chosen. Organisms most frequently isolated from wounds are listed in *Table 4.2*.

| Table 4.2: Potential wound pathogens | |
|---|---|
| **Gram-positive facultative cocci** | β-haemolytic streptocci<br>    *Streptococcus pyogenes*<br>    *Streptococcus* species (Group G) |
| | enterococci<br>    *Enterococcus faecium*<br>    *Enterococcus faecalis* |
| | staphylococci<br>    *Staphylococcus aureus*<br>    Methicillin-resistant *Staphylococcus aureus* (MRSA)<br>    *Staphylococcus epidermidis* |
| **Gram-negative aerobic rods** | *Pseudomonas aeruginosa* |
| **Gram-negative facultative rods** | *Acinetobacter* species<br>*Enterobacter* species<br>*Escherichia coli*<br>*Klebsiella* species<br>*Proteus* species<br>*Serratia marcescens* |
| **Anaerobes** | *Bacteroides* species<br>*Clostridium* species<br>*Peptostreptococcus* species<br>*Prevotella* species |
| **Fungi** | yeasts<br>    *Candida* species |
| | mycelial fungi<br>    *Aspergillus* species<br>    *Fusarium* species |

In the UK, swabs are usually collected and transported to the pathology laboratory, where potential pathogens are normally isolated, cultivated in pure culture, then characterized. Samples of pus also provide suitable material for analysis. Unfortunately, there is no simple universal regime available to recover all species in one step, and complex, time-consuming protocols have been developed.

Whereas certain pathogens are fully identified and their antibiotic sensitivities determined, complete identification of other isolates, such as coliforms, coryneforms or anaerobes, is not routinely attempted. Normal skin flora will not be identified, and total viable counts are not carried out. However, relative proportions of isolates are provided by a semi-quantitative system by reporting either +++, ++, and +, or 'heavy, moderate or light growth' from the distribution of growth on primary isolation plates. For effective wound management, this information is frequently sufficient to make correct clinical decisions. Difficulties arise if pathology reports are used to make inferences about the impact of microbes on the healing process, because comprehensive analysis of the entire microbial community in the wound is essential to make such judgements.

## Limitations of routine wound sampling

Although swabs have long been used for pathological investigations (Councilman, 1893), there are controversies surrounding their use in wounds. Standardized protocols for swabbing wounds have not been established, despite ongoing debate (Cuzzell, 1993; Cooper and Lawrence, 1996; Donovan, 1998; Gilchrist, 2000). Concerns about whether to cleanse wounds before sampling or to note (or even avoid) concurrent antimicrobial strategies when sampling remain unresolved. Variations in the absorbency of swab materials (Lawrence and Ameen, 1998), difficulties in removing adherent microbes from wounds, and uncertainties in the efficiency of recovering organisms attached to swabs (Moore and Griffith, 2002) raise questions about the reliability of swabbing.

Another problem relates to the survival of species after their removal from their natural environment because changes in local conditions may adversely affect their viability. However, not all species will react in the same way: some will be more sensitive to changed temperatures, oxygen tension, or nutritional factors, so the relative proportions of species within the wound community may start to change. The period of time and the transport conditions between sampling and processing may therefore be critical. Clinical specimens should ideally reach the laboratory within four hours of collection from the patient; ambient temperatures should be maintained; and the presence of transport media will prolong microbial viability. Nutritionally fastidious organisms, anaerobes, slow-growing organisms, and organisms present in low numbers are most difficult to recover in the laboratory.

There is a perception that densities of anaerobes in particular, may have been underestimated in previous studies because of difficulties in culturing, isolating and identifying them (Bowler *et al*, 2001; Davies *et al*, 2001). Specialist facilities and expertise are essential for the reliable characterization of anaerobes.

## Microbial culturability

Despite extensive investigations into the microbial flora of wounds during the past one hundred and twenty years, those groups of organisms that were originally discovered continue to represent those frequently isolated by modern laboratories. Coliforms, yeasts and fungi have been added to the list, and further species are only exceptionally and sporadically reported. Because few species have distinctive features that allow their recognition by microscopic analysis alone, biochemical and physiological characteristics are used.

Conventional processing of clinical specimens involves the segregation and cultivation of microorganisms in pure culture before identification begins. Growth depends on the simulation of natural conditions (the wound environment), which cannot be strictly replicated in the laboratory. Hence microbial cultivation systems could be considered artificial, and the resultant isolates unrepresentative. Ecological studies have shown that only small percentages of metabolically active species present in environmental samples are recovered in laboratory cultures (Desmonts *et al*, 1990); our inability to cultivate the bacteria that cause leprosy or syphilis illustrates the limitations of conventional systems.

Advances in the molecular techniques of gene amplification and sequencing, together with the development of an improved system of taxonomy (Woese, 1987), have provided the means to identify uncultured pathogens according to the base sequence of the 16S ribosomal RNA gene (Relman, 1993). Bacterial ribosomes contain three types of RNA molecules: 5S, 16S and 23S. Similarity in 16S ribosomal RNA genes reflects evolutionary relatedness, and is a means of identifying species. It also provides the information to update Koch's postulates (Fredricks and Relman, 1996). Application of these sophisticated approaches to investigate the complex microbial communities associated with diabetic foot ulcers and chronic leg ulcers has been attempted (Redkar *et al*, 2000 and Davies *et al*, 2001, respectively) and it is possible that new species will be discovered in the future.

## Conclusion

The exploration of microbial communities is influenced by the investigative techniques deployed. In wounds, conventional techniques are used routinely for the detection of pathogens and opportunist pathogens that may be implicated in infection. This information allows appropriate selection of antimicrobial interventions and dressings. Molecular techniques of ribotyping are costly and not likely to be used routinely, but they will allow the detection of all species present, irrespective of their culturability. In the future, they may also provide more detailed information about the composition of microbial communities, allowing for a deeper understanding of the impact of microorganisms on the healing process.

## Key points

❖ Routine analysis of clinical specimens collected from wounds aims to characterise potential pathogens and determine antibiotic susceptibilities.

❖ Conventional sampling and recovery methods have limitations.

❖ Ribotyping may provide more comprehensive information about the composition of microbial communities in wounds.

## References

Bowler PG, Davies BJ (1999a) The microbiology of acute and chronic wounds. *Wounds* **11**: 72–9

Bowler PG, Davies BJ (1999b) The microbiology of infected and non-infected wounds. *Int J Dermatol* **38**: 101–6

Bowler PG, Duerden BI, Armstrong DG (2001) Wound microbiology and associated approaches to wound management. *Clin Microbiol Rev* **14**(2): 244–69

Cooper RA, Lawrence JC (1996) The isolation and identification of bacteria from wounds. *J Wound Care* **5**(7): 335–40

Councilman WT (1893) The pathology and diagnosis of diphtheria. *Am J Med Sci* **106**: 540–52

Cuzzell JZ (1993) The right way to culture a wound. *Am J Nurs* May: 48–50

Davies C E, Wilson MJ, Hill KE, Stephens P, Hill CM, Harding KG, Thomas W (2001) Use of molecular techniques to study microbial diversity in the skin: Chronic wounds re-evaluated. *Wound Rep Regen* **9**(5): 332–40

Desmonts C, Minet J, Colwell R, Cormier M (1990) Fluorescent-antibody method useful for detecting viable but nonculturable Salmonella spp in chlorinated waste-water. *Appl Env Microbiol* **56**(5): 1448–52

Donovan S (1998) Wound infection and swabbing. *Prof Nurse***13**(11): 757–9

Fredricks DN, Relman DA (1996) Sequence-based identification of microbial pathogens: a reconsideration of Koch's postulates. *Clin Microbiol Rev* **9**(1): 18–3

Gilchrist B (2000) Taking a wound swab. *Nurs Times* **96**(4) (NT Plus): 2

Jones D (1978) Composition and differentiation of the genus Streptococcus. 1–49. In: Skinner FA, Quesnel LB, eds. *Streptococci. The Society of Applied Bacteriology Symposium Series No.7.* Academic Press, London

Lawrence JC, Ameen H (1998) Swabs and other sampling techniques. *J Wound Care***7**(5): 232–3

Moore G, Griffith C (2002) Factors influencing the recovery of microorganisms from surfaces using traditional hygiene swabbing. *Dairy Food and Environmental Sanitation* **22**: 410–21

Redkar R, Kalms J, Butler W, Krock L, McCleskey F, Salmen A, Piepmeier E Jnr, Del Vecchio V (2000) Identification of bacteria from a non-healing diabetic foot wound. *Mol Cell Probes* **14**(3): 163–9

Relman DA (1993) The identification of uncultured microbial pathogens. *J Infect Dis* **168**: 1–8

Villavicencio RT (1998) The history of blue pus. *J Am Coll Surg* **187**(2): 212–6

Willis AT (1969) *Clostridia of Wound Infection.* Butterworths, London

Woese CR (1987) Bacterial evolution. *Microbiol Rev* **51**: 221–71

# 5

# The contribution of microbial virulence to wound infection

*Rose A Cooper*

Although microorganisms such as bacteria are known to be present colonizing chronic wounds and are responsible for infections, little is known about the virulence factors of wound pathogens and how they impact on wound infection. With reference to our understanding of these mechanisms in other infected tissues it is possible to extrapolate their function to wound infection. Factors such as biofilm formation, endotoxins and exotoxins, quorum sensing and synergy all play their part in the bacterial colonization of wounds and the development of wound infection.

Microorganisms are ubiquitously and unevenly distributed throughout the environment according to their discrete growth requirements. Distribution patterns are never uniform because each species has specific requirements in terms of chemical, physical and biological factors, which can never be satisfied by all locations.

Although microorganisms show remarkable metabolic versatility, they establish themselves only in those places that best suit their requirements. They rarely exist as either single cells or pure cultures of single species, but rather as fairly stable mixed communities, embedded in sticky layers of slime as biofilms. These heterogeneous aggregates originate when cells adhere to an interface (usually solid or liquid) and grow and divide to form small clusters. Depending on local conditions, a continuing increase in numbers leads to raised levels of chemical signals that allow cell-to-cell communication (quorum sensing).

Until relatively recently microbial cells were thought to function independently, but research into bioluminescence of marine bacteria during the 1960s showed that cells within a community communicated by chemical signals and acted co-operatively depending on cell density (Rumbaugh *et al*, 1999). For Gram-negative bacteria, the signalling molecules are acyl homoserine lactones; and, for Gram-positive bacteria, peptides. Bacteria sense these chemical signals, and the number of cells within a community is detected so that when a critical cell density is exceeded, changes in gene expression are triggered. For some species, biofilm formation is initiated with collective synthesis of extracellular polymer (matrix) and the formation of complex three-dimensional structures (*Figure 5.1*; O'Toole *et al*, 2000). Cells embedded in biofilms have decreased sensitivity to antimicrobial agents. Several bacteria that are commonly isolated from wounds (eg. *Pseudomonas aeruginosa*, *Staphylococcus aureus* and *Escherichia coli*) generate biofilms in laboratory conditions, and *Pseudomonas aeruginosa* forms biofilms in a wound model (Serralta *et al*, 2001).

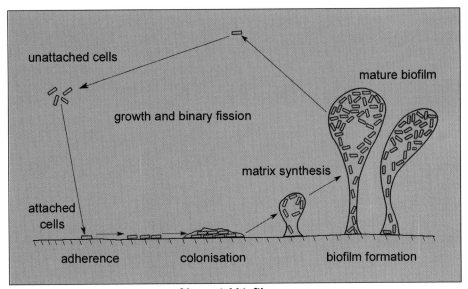

**Figure 5.1: Diagrammatic view of bacterial biofilm**

## The human body as a natural environment

The human body is host to a fairly stable collection of microbial cells that is roughly ten times larger than the total number of its constituent cells. External surfaces and cavities that open to the exterior are each colonized by a distinctive natural flora, reflecting local conditions. Organisms that derive benefit from a host without causing adverse effects comprise the majority of the natural flora, and are known as commensals. However, species with the potential to cause disease (pathogens) also contribute to natural flora. There is continuous inter-action between each host and its natural flora that results in differing outcomes at differing times. Just as pathogens can persist without causing infection, so commensals can sometimes give rise to disease. The multitude of complex influences that determine whether or not infection develops is difficult to define (Emmerson, 1998).

## Wounding

In wounding, physical barriers are breached, allowing microorganisms access to warm, moist, vulnerable tissues. Incoming species originate from: the surrounding skin; other body sites; other people; animals; or the environment. However, persistence of microorganisms in wounds is not automatic and three outcomes have been defined (Ayton, 1985). In wound contamination, the presence of incoming organisms is transient, either because suitable conditions to support their growth are not satisfied, or because host defence mechanisms prevent persistence. Alternatively, when incoming organisms find appropriate conditions for survival and can resist host defences, a balance is established and wounds become colonized without damage to the patient. Wound infection results from microbial growth, multiplication and invasion into host tissue, causing cellular injury associated with an overt immunological response. Although these outcomes are well-recognized, interaction between host and microorganisms is continuous and dynamic, and may also be viewed as a transitional spectrum (Kingsley, 2001). Definitions of wound infection vary (Leaper, 1998), but clinical indicators have been suggested (Cutting and Harding, 1994) and validated (Gardner *et al*, 2001).

## Wound bioburden

Whether or not a wound is going to develop an infection is not easy to predict. Factors that predispose a wound to bacterial invasion and infection have recently been reviewed (Heinzelmann *et al*, 2002). The size and shape of the wound, its location on the body, its duration, the presence of foreign material, and local oxygen levels are important influences on microbial survival. However, probably the greatest single influence is the immuno-competency of the patient, which is affected by several genetic and environmental factors. Nevertheless, numbers and types of microbial species are also important (*Figure 5.2*), and will be reviewed here.

One of the earliest experiences of the effects of microorganisms on wound status was by French military surgeons during World War I. They realized that wounds contaminated with high microbial loads (or any β-haemolytic streptococci) were prone to infection and best healed by secondary intention (Hepburn, 1919). Elek (1956) investigated how numbers of bacteria influenced outcomes and was able to induce pustules in normal skin by introducing 7.5 x 106 staphylococci (although lower numbers caused infection if a suture was present). Similar studies with *Pseudomonas aeruginosa* inoculated into burns created on rats showed that $10^4$ cfu/g

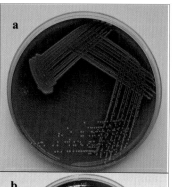

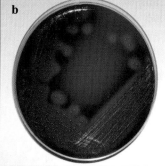

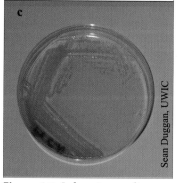

Sean Duggan, UWIC

**Figure 5.2: Laboratory cultures of three common wound infecting bacteria:**
**a. Methicillin-resistant** *Staphylococcus aureus*; **b. Streptococcus sp (Lancefield group G);**
**c.** *Pseudomonas aeruginosa*

induced tissue invasion and systemic sepsis (Teplitz *et al*, 1964) (cfu denotes 'colony-forming units', which are single microbial cells or clumps of cells that form distinct colonies when grown *in vitro*: a representation of viable counting in microbiology).

The idea of using total numbers of microorganisms as an indicator of infection was established by Kass (1957) in diagnosing pyelonephritis when numbers of bacteria in urine exceeded $10^5$/ml. This rule has been applied to wounds and it is accepted that when numbers exceed $10^5$ cfu/g or $10^5$ cfu/cm$^2$, infection is indicated (Krizek *et al*, 1967; Lookingbill *et al*, 1978; Bornside and Bornside, 1979; Raahave *et al*, 1986). The exception is in complex extremity wounds, in which $10^4$ cfu/g is the threshold (Breidenbach and Trager, 1995). Robson (1997) has discussed the need to maintain a balance in bacterial numbers to promote unimpeded healing, and deduced that numbers of less than $10^5$ cfu/g promoted granulation tissue formation, whereas higher numbers, or the presence of β-haemolytic streptococci, did not. Leg ulcers without signs of clinical infection had numbers below $10^4$ cfu/mm$^2$ and were colonized by a fairly stable microbial flora, irrespective of whether size of ulcer decreased or increased (Hansson *et al*, 1995). Since quantitative analysis of wounds is not routinely done in the UK, these thresholds are not regularly applied.

## Microbial virulence

The microbial factors that tip the balance between wound colonization and wound infection have generated much interest. *Staphylococcus aureus* is the pathogen most frequently isolated from infected wounds; yet its presence is not exclusively associated with infection (Bowler, 1998). Mertz and Ovington (1993) used an equation to represent wound infection:

$$\text{Infection} = \frac{\text{dose} \times \text{virulence}}{\text{host resistance}}$$

The virulence of a pathogen describes the extent to which it is able to cause disease. Virulence is affected by both genetic and environmental influences. A successful pathogen must invade a host, attach to its target cell, and damage host tissue without succumbing to defence mechanisms (Sharp, 1999; Wilson *et al*, 2002). Virulence is determined by the expression of multiple genes.

The first step in the development of infection is adhesion of microbial cells either to the surface of a target cell or to an extracellular matrix component. This highly specific event results from complex molecular interactions promoted by adhesins. Bacterial structures such as pili (or fimbriae) contribute to adhesion in both Gram-negative bacteria (coliforms and pseudomonads) and Gram-positive bacteria (staphylococci). Capsules assist in adhesion (streptococci, staphy-lococci, klebsiellae, pseudomonads) as well as protecting against host defences. Cell-wall components such as fibronectin binding proteins (eg. staphylococci and streptococci), protein A (staphylococci), lipoteichoic acid (staphylococci and streptococci), and lipopolysaccharides (*Escherichia coli*) also facilitate adhesion.

After attachment, some wound pathogens invade further into the wound using invasins to disrupt host tissue. Invasins are enzymes secreted by bacteria that hydrolyse components of either the extracellular matrix or intercellular connections, thereby allowing extracellular bacterial invasion away from the wound surface into deeper tissue. In staphylococci and streptococci, a range of invasins are known: hyaluronidase causes breakdown of proteoglycans in connective tissue; staphylokinase and streptokinase digest fibrin clots; and nuclease and lipase break down nucleic acids and lipids, respectively. In pseudo-monads, several proteolytic enzymes (elastases, protease IV and alkaline phosphatase) are released that attack extracellular matrix components and soluble proteins. Further injury to host tissue results from the release of bacterial toxins. Bacteria can produce endotoxins and exotoxins (*Table 5.1*). Endotoxins are embedded in the cell wall and released only on bacterial death and disruption; their effects are both local and systemic, and depend on dose. In Gram-negative bacteria, an endotoxin is lipopolysaccharide that is an integral part of the outer bacterial membrane. In Gram-positive bacteria, however, endotoxin is derived from cell wall components such as fragments of peptidoglycan and teichoic acids. In both cases, toxic effects are due to activation of pro-inflammatory responses that cause fever, diarrhoea and, in extreme cases, septic shock.

Exotoxins are usually of higher toxicity than endotoxins: they are secreted from viable bacteria and interfere with the function of specific target host cells. Many exotoxins are known and have been divided into three categories. Cytolytic toxins insert themselves into the cell membranes of specific cells and cause loss of integrity by causing pores to form (eg. haemolysins in staphy-lococci and streptococci; leukocidins in staphylococci ) or by attacking phospholipids (eg. lecithinase in *Clostridium perfringens*). A second type of exotoxin is composed of several sub-units and is known as A-B toxins. One sub-unit (B) binds to the target cell membrane and the other subunit gains entry to the cell, where it interferes with normal function. Tetanus toxin of *Clostridium tetani* is one example and exotoxin A of *Pseudomonas aeruginosa* is another. Superantigens are the third category of exotoxins. These elicit a massive inflammatory response by binding to the surface of target cells. Some strains of *Staphylococcus aureus* and *Streptococcus pyogenes* can induce toxic shock syndromes by the expression of superantigens.

Virulence determinants are many and varied, and have been the subject of several textbooks. Only a selection is presented here, and some examples are provided in *Table 5.2*. It must be remembered that the successful pathogen also has strategies to evade host defences and ensure transmission to the next susceptible host.

## Table 5.1: Examples of toxins associated with selected wound bacteria

| | Pseudomonads | Staphylococci | Streptococci |
|---|---|---|---|
| **Structure features** | Pili (adherence)<br>Alginate capsules/slime layers* (protection) | Pili (adherence)<br>Fibrinogen binding protein (adherence)<br>Protein A* (binds to IgG to prevent phagocytosis) | Fibrinogen binding protein (adherence) |
| **Invasins** | Elastase A* and B* alkaline phosphatase* and protease IV (breakdown of extracellular matrix components) | Coagulase* (protection from phagocytosis)<br>Hyaluronidase (breakdown of proteoglycans in connective tissue)<br>Staphylokinase (breakdown of fibrin clots to allow invasion)<br>Nuclease (breakdown of host nucleic acid)<br>Lipase (breakdown of host lipids) | Streptokinase (breakdown of fibrin clots)<br>Hyaluronidase (breakdown of proteoglycans in connective tissue) |
| **Toxins** | Exotoxin A* (inhibits host protein synthesis)<br>Phospholipase C* (haemolysis) | Leukocidin (destroys leukocytes) α and β-toxins (haemolysis)<br>γ-toxin (kills cells)<br>δ-toxin (haemolysis and leukolysis) | Streptolysin O (haemolysis)<br>Streptolysin S (haemolysis) |

* expression subject to quorum sensing

## Regulation of virulence determinants and quorum sensing

Microorganisms have effective means of detecting changes in environmental conditions and responding to them. Metabolic function is controlled either by changing the activity of existing enzymes, or by controlling the synthesis of proteins by regulating gene expression. Virulence determinants are subject to genetic as well as to environmental influences. The mechanisms that allow the evolution of pathogens and the regulation virulence genes have been reviewed by Wilson *et al* (2002), yet the importance of microbial numbers in modulating bacterial function has not yet been explained. Researchers realize now that quorum sensing is involved not only in biofilm formation, but also in the control of virulence factors in certain pathogens (*Table 5.2*). Certain bacterial species present in wounds are therefore less virulent in low numbers than in high ones. In *Pseudomonas aeruginosa*, quorum sensing is important in regulating the virulence of strains that cause burn infections (Van Delden and Iglewski, 1998; Rumbaugh *et al*, 1999). Quorum sensing also contributes to the regulation of exotoxins and extracellular enzymes in *Staphylococcus aureus* and *Streptococcus pyogenes* (Dunny and Leonard, 1997; Miller and Bassler, 2001).

| Table 5.2: Bacterial virulence factors: an outline of action | | |
|---|---|---|
| | **Endotoxin** | **Exotoxin** |
| **Location** | In the cell wall; masked in viable cells but released on cell lysis | Extracellular toxins, secreted by viable cells |
| **Chemistry** | Lipopolysaccharide in Gram-negative bacteria | Protein |
| **Effects** | Systemic effects depend on concentration | Toxins exert their effects on specific target cells |
| **Toxicity** | Usually low | Depends on the toxin, but can be high |

## Conclusion

In certain wound pathogens, virulence is modulated by cell-to-cell signals that are dependent on cell density. The expression of some adhesins, invasins and toxins is affected by quorum sensing, and further research into this aspect of wound infection is needed. At present, biofilm formation has been reported in a wound model (Serralta *et al*, 2001); it is likely that biofilms form in wounds. If so, this might account for wound chronicity because cells in biofilms have reduced susceptibility to antimicrobial agents and host immunological mechanisms, as well as raised virulence. Elsewhere, they have been implicated in persistent infections (Costerton *et al*, 1999). Our thinking about the significance of the microbial bioburden of wounds may require some revision. Perhaps total numbers of microorganisms are less significant than numbers of particular species which have the potential of quorum sensing to improve their virulence and persistence. Already the importance of eradicating streptococci before skin grafting is recognized (Schraibman, 1990). Future strategies in wound management may revolve around the detection, enumeration and reduction of 'rogue' species.

## Key points

❖ Microorganisms are often associated with wounds, but whether they establish colonisation or infection is dependent on complex interactions between the patient and the microbial community.

❖ Immunocompetency of the patient affects the development of wound infection.

❖ Microbial numbers can influence the expression of virulence genes in certain species by quorum sensing.

❖ Interactions between different types of microorganisms (synergy) may influence the development of wound infection.

# References

Ayton M (1985) Wounds that won't heal. *Nurs Times* **81**(46 suppl): 16–19

Bornside GH, Bornside BB (1979) Comparison between moist swab and tissue biopsy methods for bacteria in experimental incision wounds. *J Trauma* **19**: 103–5

Bowler P (1998) The anaerobic and aerobic microbiology of wounds: a review. *Wounds* **10**(6): 170–8

Breidenbach WC, Trager S (1995) Quantitative culture technique and infection in complex wounds of the extremities closed with free flaps. *Plast Reconstr Surg* **95**: 860–5

Costerton JW, Stewart PS, Greenberg EP (1999) Bacterial biofilms: a common cause of persistent infections. *Science* **284**: 1318–22

Cutting KF, Harding KG (1994) Criteria for identifying wound infection. *J Wound Care* **3**(4): 198–201

Dunny GM, Leonard BAB (1997) Cell-cell communication in Gram-positive bacteria. *Annu Rev Microbiol* **51**: 527–64

Elek SD (1956) Experimental staphylococcal infections in the skin of man. *Ann N Y Acad Sci* **65**: 85–90

Emmerson M (1998) A microbiologist's view of factors contributing to infection. *New Horiz* **6**(2): 85–90

Gardner SE, Frantz RA, Doebbeling BN (2001) The validity of the clinical signs and symptoms used to identify localised wound infection. *Wound Repair Regen* **9**(3): 178–86

Hansson C, Holborn J, Moller A, Swanbeck G (1995) The microbial flora in venous leg ulcers without clinical signs of infection. *Acta Derm Venereol (Stockh)* **75**: 24–30

Heinzelmann M, Scott M, Lam T (2002) Factors predisposing to bacterial invasion and infection. *Am J Surg* **183**: 179–90

Hepburn HH (1919) Delayed primary suture of wounds. *Br Med J* **1**: 181–3

Kass EH (1957) Bacteriuria and diagnosis of infections of the urinary tract. *Arch Int Med* **100**: 709–14

Kingsley A (2001) A proactive approach to wound infection. *Nurs Stand* **15**: 50–8

Krizek TJ, Robson MC, Kho E (1967) Bacterial growth and skin graft. *Surg Forum* **18**: 518–9

Leaper D (1998) Defining infection. *J Wound Care* **7**(8): 373

Lookingbill DP, Miller SH, Knowles RC (1978) Bacteriology of chronic leg ulcers. *Arch Surg* **114**: 1765–8

Mertz PM, Ovington LG (1993) Wound healing microbiology. *Dermatol Clin* **11**(4): 739–47

Miller MB, Bassler BL (2001) Quorum sensing in bacteria. *Annu Rev Microbiol* **55**: 165–99

O'Toole G, Kaplan HB, Kolter R (2000) Biofilm formation as microbial development. *Annu Rev Microbiol* **54**: 49–79

Raahave D, Friis-Moller A, Bjerre-Jespen K, Rasmussen LB (1986) The infective dose of aerobic and anaerobic bacteria in post-operative wound sepsis. *Arch Surg* **121**: 924–9

Robson MC (1997) Wound infection a failure of wound healing caused by an imbalance of bacteria. *Surg Clin North Am* **77**(3): 637–50

Rumbaugh KP, Griswold JA, Iglewski BH, Hamood AN (1999) Contribution of quorum sensing to the virulence of *Pseudomonas aeruginosa* in burn wound infections. *Infect Immun* **67**: 5854–62

Schraibman IG (1990) The significance of beta-haemolytic streptococci in chronic leg ulcers. *Ann R Coll Surg Engl* **72**(2): 123–4

Serralta AW, Harrison-Balestra C, Cazzaniga AL, Davis S, Mertz PM (2001) Lifestyles of bacteria in wounds: presence of biofilms? *Wounds* **13**(1): 29–34

Sharp SE (1999) Commensal and pathogenic micro-organisms of humans. In: Murray PR, Baron EJ, Pfaller MA, Tenover FC, Yolken RH, eds. *Manual of Clinical Microbiology*. 7th edn. ASM Press, Washington DC

Teplitz C, Davis D, Mason AD, Moncrief JA (1964) *Pseudomonas aeruginosa* burn wound sepsis. *J Surg Res* **4**: 200–16

Van Delden C, Iglewski BH (1998) Cell-to-cell signalling and *Pseudomonas aeruginosa* infections. *Emerg Infect Dis* **4**(4): 551–60

Wilson JW, Schurr MJ, LeBlanc CL, Ramamurthy R, Buchana KL, Nickerson CA (2002) Mechanisms of bacterial pathogenicity. *Postgrad Med J* **78**: 216–24

# 6

# The use of topical antimicrobials in wound bioburden control

*Richard J White, Rose A Cooper*

The control of wound bioburden is believed to be valuable in avoiding possible deterioration into infection; in reducing critical colonization; and in treating frank infection. While the immune response is the governing factor in the development of infection, the reduction of bioburden — if achieved to a sufficient degree and for sufficient duration — can enable host defences to regain control. Topical anti-microbial agents, carefully selected and correctly dosed, can help achieve these goals. This review examines the value of topical antiseptics and antibiotics in various formulations in controlling the bioburden of acute and, predominantly, chronic wounds. The currently held perception of antibiotic misuse is reinforced and reiterated. Topical antibiotics must be used with caution and only for specific, limited indications. Topical antiseptics have a much broader range of applications and are generally safer when used appropriately. Conditions and circumstances of use are provided for these agents.

Whether or not microorganisms survive in a wound depends on their ability to evade the body's immune response, and whether their essential chemical and physical requirements for survival are met. Contaminating organisms may not persist, but those species that do grow and divide may establish either wound colonization or wound infection (*Figure 6.1*). The presence of microorganisms in a wound is not unusual. Chronic wounds are usually colonized by large numbers of bacteria (Dale *et al*, 1983; Brook and Frazier, 1990; Brook, 1991). These wounds do not always develop infection (Bowler *et al*, 2001) and many continue to heal despite being colonized (Cooper *et al*, 2002). The development of infection in chronic wounds often reflects host susceptibility (Bowler *et al*, 2001; Heinzelmann *et al*, 2002).

As elective (ie. surgical) wounds are subject to rigorous preoperative antiseptic measures and aseptic surgical techniques, infection is minimized and healing often proceeds within the expected time frame. Traumatic wounds are more likely to contain devitalised tissue and debris, and to be contaminated with microorganisms from environmental sources. Consequently, infection rates are higher.

Wound infection is one of the most significant factors that delays healing. Although a consensus about the impact of specific microorganisms on the healing process has yet to be agreed, the development of an infection causes serious delays in healing. Additional effects for the patient may be increased pain and discomfort; loss of income; inconvenience; and even life-threatening illness.

Adverse effects on the healthcare system may be an extended hospital stay and increased treatment costs in terms of extra antibiotic and dressings usage, together with extra staff costs.

The increased use of antibiotics has caused the emergence of antibiotic resistant strains (Kelly, 2001). This is a matter of concern, particularly as there is indiscriminate and clinically unjustified use of antibiotics (Levy, 1998; Kelly, 2001).

Among healthcare professionals, there is increasing concern about the risks associated with the presence of microorganisms in wounds: do they represent a real risk for cross-infection? Should antimicrobial agents be used — if so, when?

**Antibiotic**

A chemical substance produced by a microorganism, which has the capacity, in dilute solutions, to inhibit selectively the growth (static) of microorganisms or to kill (cidal) them.

**Disinfectant**

A non-selective agent that disinfects by killing or removing microorganisms from inert surfaces, used particularly on medical instruments, work surfaces, etc. They are not intended for use on the tissues of the body where toxicity would impair healing.

**Antiseptic**

A disinfectant substance that can be used on skin and on wounds that either kills (cidal) or prevents the multiplication (static) of potentially pathogenic organisms. Antiseptics can be dilute disinfectants; they are not selective and therefore can be toxic to the host tissue, particularly at higher concentrations. Antiseptics have the advantage of rarely selecting for resistant microbial strains, and, being topical, do not rely on the bloodstream for access to the wound; this is particularly important in ischaemic wounds (Saffle and Schnebly, 1994). However, they have the possible disadvantage of toxicity to the tissues at higher concentrations (Scott Ward and Saffle, 1995).

**Bioburden**

The microbial loading of the skin and/or wounds with normal commensals and potential pathogens.

**Colonization**

The presence of multiplying bacteria with no overt host (immunological) reaction (Ayton, 1985) or clinical symptoms. This definition currently applies irrespective of the numbers and species of organisms in the wound.

**Critical colonization**

The situation in which host defences cannot maintain the balance of organisms in a wound (White *et al*, 2002).

**Infection**

The presence of multiplying bacteria in body tissues, resulting in the spread of cellular injury due to competitive metabolism, toxins, intracellular replication, or antigen-antibody response (host reaction). This would be apparent from any one or more of the classical signs of inflammation: erythema, heat, swelling, pain. The accepted diagnostic criteria for wound infection are those defined by Cutting and Harding (1994).

**Figure 6.1: Definitions**

## Preventative measures

Measures to prevent wound infection and delayed healing situations are based on sound tissue viability principles, which have been outlined by White *et al* (2001).

## Therapeutic measures

Active steps taken to reduce colonization or to counter infection depend on the nature of the wound, the health status of the patient and the pathogenicity of the organism(s) involved. Clearly, an organ-transplant patient threatened with a methicillin-resistant *Staphylococcus aureus* (MRSA) infection in their surgical wound is at greater risk than a patient with a long-standing leg ulcer that is colonized, because the immunosuppression of the former puts him or her at higher risk of life-threatening infection. The bacterial loading or bioburden of the wound may influence the healing rate and is a particularly important factor in patients who are 'at risk', eg. those who have compromised healing or host response, diabetes and/or ischaemia.

Antimicrobial agents have been applied to wounds for thousands of years (Moellering, 1995), but the relentless emergence of resistant strains has forced the continued search for novel agents. As each new type of antimicrobial agent has been discovered and introduced into clinical practice, changes in microbial sensitivity have occurred. At the outset, there are always some strains that are not inhibited by a new agent (ie. they possess intrinsic resistance) and some species that are susceptible. A new antimicrobial agent limits the growth of susceptible strains, but eventually resistant strains always emerge. These agents do not induce the formation of resistance genes, but merely provide an environment in which sensitive species are curtailed and resistant species flourish.

Resistance can arise by mutation and also by the exchange of resistance genes between resistant and non-resistant strains. Cases of resistance genes that confer multiple resistance have also been discovered (Collis and Hall, 1995). The emergence of wound pathogens with patterns of multiple antibiotic resistance is having serious consequences in the hospital environment (Morgan *et al*, 2000); nursing homes (Fraise *et al*, 1997); and in the community (Moreno *et al*, 1995). The situation is compounded by the increasing costs of searching for new antimicrobials and the decreasing rate of discovery of new agents (Moellering, 1995).

### Antibiotics

Guidelines for the correct use of antibiotics have been defined (Kelly, 2001; Berendt and Lipskay, 2003). Appropriate systemic antibiotics are deemed essential for the treatment of clinically infected wounds (Bowler *et al*, 2001).

The use of topical antibiotics, however, should be avoided in most cases (Gould and Brooker, 2000) and is not justified for the routine treatment of colonized or infected wounds (*Drug and Therapeutics Bulletin*, 1991). Topical antibiotics can provoke delayed hypersensitivity reactions (Zaki *et al*, 1994); superinfections (infection by resistant bacteria); and, more importantly, selection for resistance (*British Medical Journal*, 1977). Selection for resistance is more likely with antibiotics that are used both topically and systemically — eg. gentamicin, metronidazole, sodium fusidate, chlortetracycline and others. Only mupirocin and metronidazole are justified for topical use — and then only in restricted indications.

There is evidence that the routine use of antibiotics in the management of clinically infected leg ulcers is of no benefit (Alinovi *et al*, 1986) and some evidence that it may even be harmful by encouraging colonization by resistant organisms (Huovinen and Kotilainen, 1994). Resistance to antibiotics has become a serious problem for those involved in wound care; the situation has been described as 'crisis' in the USA (Colsky *et al*, 1998).

## Antiseptics

Although clinicians used to believe that the development of resistance to antiseptics and disinfectants was a remote possibility, this belief has been shown to be untrue (McDonnell and Russell, 1999). Certain species such as myco-bacteria and Gram-negative bacteria, as well as bacterial spores, possess intrinsic resistance, but plasmid-mediated acquired resistance to antiseptics and disinfectants in several bacteria has been reported (McDonnell and Russell, 1999). Antiseptics and disinfectants have long been the cornerstone of effective infection control and the prevention of hospital-acquired infection, so the development of resistance to triclosan by MRSA is likely to have important consequences for clinical practice (Suller and Russell, 2000).

The effects of antiseptic solutions on the microbial flora of venous leg ulcers have been investigated (Hansson and Faergemann, 1995). A fifteen-minute exposure to four different antiseptic solutions on wet dressings did not alter the diversity of microbial species associated with ulcers. Although decreases in the mean number of bacteria per ulcer occurred for all the antiseptics tested, few gave statistically significant reductions. Inactivation of the antiseptics by proteins contained in ulcer exudate was the possible explanation of these disappointing inhibitory effects.

The value and use of topical antiseptics in wound care have been debated for many years. In the UK in particular, use of hypochlorites such as Edinburgh University solution of lime (EUSOL) is controversial (Moore, 1992). The consensus on EUSOL, especially among nurses, is that it has no place in wound care, irrespective of the concentration used (Roe *et al*, 1994). This view is based on evidence that EUSOL is rapidly deactivated in the presence of pus; is painful to the patient; and delays healing by damaging cells and capillaries (Leaper, 1988). Iodine compounds have also attracted criticism (Rodeheaver, 1990). The main objection to their use is their potential toxicity (Lawrence, 1998a), which is related to concentration and exposure and the concomitant delay in healing compared with untreated controls (Brennan and Leaper, 1985).

## Clinical evidence for the use of topical antiseptics

Careful and objective review of the literature reveals that the use of many antiseptics in wound management depends on a risk-benefit assessment of possible local toxicity with beneficial antibacterial action (Kaye, 2000). Brennan and Leaper (1985) advised balancing the beneficial antimicrobial effects and bioavailability with possible cellular toxicity before usage.

In solution form, antiseptics are often used to irrigate or cleanse the wound — which necessarily requires a short period of contact with the tissues. Solutions are concentrated, therefore, to have the correct effect, which increases the likelihood of tissue toxicity and delayed healing. Antiseptic agents incorporated into dressings are in contact with the wound for much longer, and can be more diluted, less toxic, and exert an extended antimicrobial effect.

The ideal antiseptic will have the following key attributes (summarized from Morison, 1990):

- broad spectrum of activity
- low potential for resistance
- non-toxic to white blood cells in the early inflammatory stage and later to fibroblasts and keratinocytes
- rapid acting
- neither an irritant nor a sensitizer
- effective even in the presence of exudate, pus, slough, etc.

### Iodine

Iodine was first used in 1839 by Davies as an aqueous potassium iodine solution for the treatment of wounds. It was evaluated by both Pasteur and Koch, and used extensively in the American Civil War (Hugo, 1991). Alcoholic tinctures of iodine and iodoform have long been used in wound care, but these early products had limited value in modern wound care because of the pain and staining that they caused. The development of povidone-iodine (a polyvinyl pyrrolidone surfactant/iodine complex or PVP-I) in 1949 and, later, cadexomer iodine (a three-dimensional starch lattice containing iodine) has provided safer, less painful alternatives that function by the sustained release of low concentrations of free iodine. The efficacy of PVP-I as a pre-surgical skin antiseptic is unquestioned, but its value in wound care has been extensively debated (Thomas, 1988; Rodeheaver, 1990; Goldenheim, 1993; Lawrence, 1998a/b; Gulliver, 1999). Concerns about toxicity and impaired healing related mainly to the older products that contained free elemental iodine, but PVP-I has been criticized (Kramer, 1999), contrary to the opinion of the Food and Drug

Administration in the USA that maintains that PVP-I in 5–10% solutions does not adversely affect healing (Federal Register, 1994). In *in vitro* tests, PVP-I has demonstrated cidal activity against a broad range of species including antibiotic resistant strains (McLure and Gordon, 1992; Traoré *et al*, 1996; Kunisada *et al*, 1997; Lanker Klossner *et al*, 1997; Payne *et al*, 1999; Rikimaru *et al*, 2002; Giacometti *et al*, 2002).

Iodine, as an iodophor, is available in a range of concentrations as medicated dressings (eg. Inadine[1]; Iodoflex[2]), solutions and ointments (eg. Betadine[3]), powder and spray (eg. Savlon[4] Dry powder), and incise drapes (Ioban[5]). The cadexomer is a polysaccharide starch lattice containing 0.9% elemental iodine that is released on exposure to exudate (Lawrence, 1998a), and is available as Iodosorb[6]. It has antimicrobial activity for up to three days (Mertz *et al*, 1999). It has been extensively evaluated in a variety of acute and chronic wounds and found to be safe and effective (Sundberg and Meller, 1997). Moreover, Moore *et al* (1997) suggested that because Iodosorb modulates macrophages *in vitro*, it may enhance healing *in vivo*, and Zhou *et al* (2002) showed cadexomer iodine to be non-toxic for fibroblasts *in vitro*. Hence, these newer iodine products are considered of value in modern wound care (Gilchrist, 1997a/b).

Unlike other antimicrobial agents with a long history of usage, there is only limited evidence of the emergence of iodine-resistant strains to date (Mycock, 1985). The non-specific mode of action of iodine in affecting multiple cellular functions (Gottardi, 1983) probably accounts for this outcome.

## Silver

Silver and silver compounds have been routinely used as bactericidals for many years (see *Chapter 7* [White, 2001]; Klasen, 2000). Silver is generally recognised as a safe, broad-spectrum agent with only irritation and skin discolouration (argyria) reported for the inorganic nitrate solution (Wright *et al*, 1998). The mode of action has been reported (Russell and Hugo, 1994).

The chemical bonding of silver with a sulphonamide antimicrobial, sulphadiazine (silver sulphadiazine or SSD) has resulted in a safe, broad-spectrum agent for topical use. Silver is released slowly from the oil-in-water cream formulation in concentrations that are selectively toxic to microorganisms such as bacteria (MRSA, gentamicin-resistant pseudomonads and enterococci) and fungi (Mandell and Sande, 1990).

SSD has been a mainstay of topical burns therapy (Pruitt, 1987) and has been used successfully in acute (Buckley *et al*, 2000) and chronic wounds (Bishop *et al*, 1992) to treat infection. Resistance to SSD has occurred (Modak

1    Trademark of Johnson & Johnson Wound Management
2    Trademark of Smith & Nephew
3    Trademark of SSL
4    Trademark of Novartis
5    Trademark of 3M
6    Trademark of Smith & Nephew

and Fox, 1981), but it is rare. A range of topical silver preparations has been assessed on chronic wounds (O'Meara *et al*, 2000, 2001) in controlled trials with generally favourable results.

Recently, several silver-containing dressings have become available (*Chapter 7*). In any formulation, the way in which silver is incorporated and how it interacts with microorganisms — ie. its bioavailability in solution — is critical in assessing its antimicrobial efficiency and its safety (Demling and DeSanti, 2001). Actisorb Silver 220 (Johnson and Johnson Medical) contains silver absorbed into an activated charcoal cloth (Williams, 1994). It is effective against a wide range of microorganisms (Furr *et al*, 1994). There are several reports of clinical data to support the clinical efficacy of Actisorb Silver 220 (*Chapter 8* [Scanlon and Dowsett, 2001]; *Chapter 7* [White, 2001]; Leak, 2002). Acticoat film (Smith & Nephew, UK) is an antimicrobial barrier dressing that is also effective against a wide range of organisms (Yin *et al*, 1999). Although the delivery systems vary, the mode of action principle is the same in each case. The currently available silver containing dressings are ascribed with different characteristics of silver bioavailability, whilst this is clearly manifested in *in vitro* assays it does not appear to correlate with clinical performance. Thus, dressings which make silver available to the tissues (ie. bioavailable) are not necessarily more or less effective than those dressings which retain silver within their structure. The most important parameters for clinical efficacy are the interaction of bacteria with silver and the duration of the effect.

## Honey

Honey is an ancient wound remedy (Jones, 2001) that is accredited with many curative properties (Molan, 1998). Antibacterial activity has been demonstrated by numerous *in vitro* studies (Molan, 1992, Willix *et al*, 1992; Cooper and Molan, 1999; Cooper *et al*, 1999 and 2001). Clinical evidence is from case studies (Dunford *et al*, 2000; Natarajan *et al*, 2001; Cooper *et al*, 2001), cohort studies and clinical trials (Molan, 1999), but has been criticised (Moore *et al*, 2001). Mechanisms by which honey influences the healing process are not yet fully explained (Tonks *et al*, 2001; Tonks *et al*, 2003).

## Proflavine

Proflavine is an acridine derivative (a compound originally used in the manufacture of dyes). It is available as a cream British Pharmaceutical Codex (BPC), solution BPC and as the hemisulphate, and has been in use for many years as a slow-acting, mildly bacteriostatic agent — ie. it inhibits bacterial growth — in wound management. In particular, proflavine is still widely used as a gauze soak for surgical wound packing, even though it has been reported to be inferior to an alginate dressing in this respect (Gupta *et al*, 1991). There is no reliable evidence that proflavine is effective as an impregnated gauze, or that it has any clinical benefits. Indeed, there are reports that proflavine has been responsible for gene and chromosomal mutations in bacterial cultures (Iwamoto *et al*,

1992) and cell cultures (DeMarini *et al*, 1988), raising doubts about its safety.

## Chlorhexidine compounds

These are useful antiseptics for skin because they are highly effective for hand-washing and for surgical scrub. They bind to the skin surface and have a persistent activity, remaining active for at least six hours after application (Kaye, 2000). The acetate form, Chlorasept™ (Baxter), is indicated for wound irrigation. The gluconate form is active against Gram-negative organisms such as *Pseudomonas aeruginosa* and Gram-positive ones such as *Staphylococcus aureus* and *Escherichia coli*. The toxicity and safety for use on wounds of chlorhexidine has not been established categorically, but it may be a useful therapeutic option as an agent for topical use (Scott Ward and Saffle, 1995).

## Wound dressings

The use of modern dressings in bioburden and infection control shows great promise. Medicated dressings (containing silver and iodine) can be useful in local control of bacterial bioburden provided the active agents — silver ions and elemental iodine — are bioavailable at an appropriate concentration over time. Such dressings will, in turn, assist in infection control by reducing the numbers of wound pathogens available for cross-infection.

Dressings containing antibiotics have a diminishing place in wound treatment, primarily due to resistance. However, a case can be made for the use of topical mupirocin in the elimination of nasal carriage of *Staphylococcus aureus*, and for metronidazole gel in the palliative treatment of malodorous malignant (fungating) wounds in which odour is a major problem (Rice, 1992).

## Chronic wounds

The detailed reviews by O'Meara *et al* (2000, 2001) and the Scottish Intercollegiate Guidelines Network (SIGN, 1998) have found little evidence to support the routine use of systemic antibiotics in patients with chronic wounds.

Acute and spreading infections in chronic wounds should, however, be treated with systemic antibiotics (Bowler *et al*, 2001). Topical dressings, creams or ointments that provide sufficient delivery of an antiseptic agent (eg. silver or iodine) may be useful (White *et al*, 2001). However, the use in solution of povidone-iodine as a wound cleanser is not appropriate (Leaper, 1988; Burks, 1998). Solutions of antimicrobials, when used as wound rinses, do not have sufficiently long contact times to have much effect in reducing bacterial numbers.

## Surgical wounds

Clean surgery carries a small (1–5%) risk of postoperative wound infection, whereas 'dirty procedures' such as those involving the large intestines have a much higher risk (up to 27%; Nichols, 1998). The minimizing of the incidence of infection relies on adequate asepsis, antisepsis and preservation of local host defences (Hunt, 1981). Asepsis involves effective infection control to minimize exogenous contamination during surgery. Antisepsis involves skin antiseptics and prophylactic antibiotics before surgery (Hansis, 1996). Recent guidelines on the prevention of surgical site infection have been published (Mangram *et al*, 1999). The emphasis on surgical wound healing is rapid perfusion as ischaemic tissue heals poorly and is easily infected (Hunt and Hopf, 1997). Healing and resistance to infection improve with increased local blood supply, and hence tissue oxygenation.

Delivery of antibiotics, systemically dosed, to the infected wound also depends on perfusion. Antibiotics given at the time of injury will reduce, but not eliminate, the risk of infection.

In one third of wound infections, bacteria cultured from the wound are susceptible to the prophylactic antibiotic provided; the key factors involved here are patients with hypoxia and local perfusion problems (Hunt and Hopf, 1997). In such instances, it is easy to make a case for prophylactic and therapeutic antiseptics — particularly those provided by sustained dosing from 'medicated' dressings.

## Conclusion

It is time to reassess our approach to wound bioburden and its control, as the emergence of wound pathogens with patterns of multiple antibiotic resistance is having serious consequences in all healthcare situations. Antibiotic, antiseptic and antimicrobial use must be selective, appropriate and proportionate.

There is strong evidence that the presence of different species of micro-organisms in the wound can be linked to delayed healing and wound odour. When overt infection exists, systemic antibiotics are usually an appropriate first-line treatment; topical treatments, such as antibacterial dressings, are useful adjuncts, particularly in the event of poor perfusion. Non-healing wounds in which critical colonization is suspected or confirmed may also be appropriate for such treatment.

In the case of silver as an antiseptic, the antibacterial action and effects on indolent wounds (Demling and DeSanti, 2001) and burns (Wright *et al*, 1999) have been established. Silver can 'provide a disinfected surface in the immediate environment of the wound, thus preventing bacterial infection' (Gilchrist, 1997; cited in Williams, 1997). For iodine as iodophor or cadexomer preparations, the consensus is in favour of its use in non-healing and infected chronic wounds (Gilchrist, 1997a; Sundberg and Meller, 1997). Once the infection or critical colonization is reduced and the wound shows signs of healing, the dressing should be changed for one that is appropriate to the wound.

Antiseptics and disinfectants have long been the cornerstone of effective infection control and the prevention of hospital-acquired infection. The use of topical sustained-release formulations that contain iodine or silver on infected and critically colonized wounds is justified. The indications for use of a topical antiseptic sustained delivery system — whether it be dressing, cream or ointment — are numerous. If there is one or more overt signs of infection, or any less overt signs (such as increased exudate levels, increased local pain, or cessation of progress in healing), intervention is indicated to return the wound to health. The use of appropriate topical products will also assist in the reduction of odour and local bioburden, so reducing the risks of cross infection.

## Key points

❖ Rinsing wounds with antiseptic solutions is of no proven clinical value.

❖ Pre-treatment of the skin with appropriate antiseptics is an important procedure in reducing the risk of surgical wound infection.

❖ Topical antibiotics are of very limited value in treating infected wounds; they should be used with great caution and only when there is no alternative.

❖ Systemic antibiotics, dosed appropriately, are indicated for overt infection with signs of spreading cellulitis.

❖ Dressings and other delivery systems that deliver sustained doses of effective antimicrobials, such as silver and iodine, have been shown to be valuable in the treatment of critical colonisation and infection.

## References

Alinovi A, Bassissi P, Pini M (1986) Systemic administration of antibiotics in the management of venous ulcers. *J Am Acad Dermatol* **15**: 186–91

Ayton M (1985) Wounds that won't heal. *Nurs Times* **81**(46): 16–9

Berendt T, Lipskay BA (2003) Should antibiotics be used in the treatment of the diabetic foot? *The Diabetic Foot* **6**(1): 18–28

Bishop JB, Phillips LG, Mustoe TA *et al* (1992) A prospective randomised evaluator-blinded trial of two potential wound healing agents for the treatment of venous stasis ulcers. *J Vasc Surg* **16**(2): 251–7

Bowler PG, Duerden BI, Armstrong DG (2001) Wound microbiology and associated approaches to wound management. *Clin Micro Rev* **14**(2): 244–69

Brennan SS, Leaper DJ (1985) The effect of antiseptics on the healing wound. *Br J Surg* **72**: 780–2

British Medical Journal (1977) Topical antibiotics (editorial). *Br Med J* **1**(6075): 1494

Brook I, Frazier EH (1990) Aerobic and anaerobic bacteriology of wounds and cutaneous abscesses. *Arch Surg* **125**: 1445–51

Brook I (1991) Microbiology studies on decubitus ulcers. *J Paed Surg* **26**: 207–9

Buckley SC, Scott K, Das K (2000) Late review of the use of silver sulphadiazine dressing for the treatment of fingertip injuries. *Injury* **31**: 301–4

Burks RI (1998) Povidone-iodine solution in wound treatment. *Phys Ther* **78**: 212–8

Collis CM, Hall RM (1995) Expression of antibiotic resistance genes in the integrated cassettes of intergrons. *Antimicrob Agents Chemother* **39**: 155–62

Colsky AS, Kisner R, Kerdel F (1998) Analysis of antibiotic susceptibilities of skin flora in hospitalised dermatology patients. The crisis of antibiotic resistance has come to the surface. *Arch Dermatol* **134**: 1006–9

Cooper R, Molan P (1999) The use of honey as an antiseptic in managing Pseudomonas infections. *J Wound Care* **8**(4): 161–4

Cooper RA, Molan PC, Harding KG (1999) Antibacterial activity of honey against strains of *Staphylococcus aureus* from infected wounds. *J Roy Soc Med* **92**: 283–5

Cooper RA, Molan PC, Krishnamoorthy L, Harding KG (2001) Manuka honey used to heal a recalcitrant surgical wound. *Eur J Clin Microbiol Infect Dis* **20**: 758–9

Cooper R, Kingsley A, White RJ (2002) *Wound infection and microbiology*. Institute of Wound Management monograph, Medical Communications, Cornwall

Cutting KF, Harding KG (1994) Criteria for identifying wound infection. *J Wound Care* **3**(4): 198–201

Dale JJ, Callam MJ, Ruckley CV, Harper DR, Berry PN (1983) Chronic ulcers of the leg: a study of prevalence in a Scottish community. *Health Bull* **41**: 310–4

DeMarini DM, Brock KH, Doerr CL, Moore MM (1988) Mutagenicity and clastogenicity of proflavin in L5178Y/TK cells. *J Mutat Res* **204**(2): 323–8

Demling RH, DeSanti L (2001) The role of silver in wound healing. Part 1: Effects of silver on wound management. *Wounds* **13**(1 Suppl): A3–A15

Drug and Therapeutics Bulletin (1991) Local applications to wounds: 1. Cleansers, antibacterials, debriders. *Drug Ther Bull* **29**(24): 93–5

Dunford C, Cooper R, Molan P, White RJ (2000) The use of honey in wound management. *Nurs Standard* **15**(11): 63–8

Fraise AP, Mitchell K, O'Brien SJ *et al* (1997) Methicillin-resistant *Staphylococcus aureus* in nursing homes in a major UK city: an anonymised point prevalence study. *Epidemiol Infect* **118**: 1–5

Furr JR, Russell AD, Turner TD, Andrews A (1994) Antibacterial activity of Actisorb Plus, Actisorb and silver nitrate. *J Hosp Infect* **27**: 201–8

Giacometti A, Cirioni O, Greganti G, Fineo A, Ghiselli R, Del Prete MS, Mocchegiani F, Fileni B, Caselli F, Petrelli E, Saba V, Scalise G (2002) Antiseptic compounds still active against strains isolated from surgical wound infections despite increasing antibiotic resistance. *Eur J Clin Microbiol Infect Dis* **21**: 553–6

Gilchrist B (1997a) Should iodine be reconsidered in wound management? *J Wound Care* **6**(3): 148–50

Gilchrist B (1997b) Wound infection. In: Miller M, Glover D, eds. *Wound Management*. NT Books, London

Goldenheim PD (1993) An appraisal of povidone-iodine and wound healing. *Postgrad Med J* **69**(Suppl): S97–S105

Gottardi (1983) Iodine and iodine compounds. In: Seymour Block, ed. *Disinfection, Sterilisation and Preservation*. 3rd edn. Lea Febinger, Philadelphia

Gould D, Brooker C (2000) *Applied Microbiology for Nurses*. MacMillan, London

Gulliver G (1999) Arguments over iodine. *Nurs Times* **95**(27): 68–70

Gupta R, Foster ME, Miller E (1991) Calcium alginate in the management of acute surgical wounds and abscesses. *J Tissue Viability* **1**(4): 115–6

Hansson C, Faergemann J (1995) The effect of antiseptic solutions on micro-organisms in venous leg ulcers. *Acta Derm Venereol* (Stockh) **75**: 31–3

Hansis M (1996) Pathophysiology of infection: a theoretical approach. *Injury* **27**: C5–C8

Heinzelmann M, Scott M, Lam T (2002) Factors predisposing to bacterial invasion and infection. *Am J Surg* **183**: 179–90

Hugo WB (1991) A brief history of heat and chemical preservation and disinfection. *J Appl Bacteriology* **71**: 9–18

Hunt TK (1981) Surgical wound infections: an overview. *Am J Med* **70**: 712–8

Hunt TK, Hopf HW (1997) Wound healing and wound infection. What surgeons and anaesthesiologists can do. *Surg Clin North Am* **77**(3): 587–606

Huovinen S, Kotilainen P (1994) Comparison of cyprofloxacin or trimethoprim therapy for venous leg ulcers: results of a pilot study. *J Am Acad Dermatol* **31**: 279–81

Iwamoto Y, Ferguson LR, Pearson A, Baguley BC (1992) Photo-enhancement of the mutagenicity of 9-anilinoacridine derivatives related to the antitumour agent amsacrine. *J Mutat Res* **268**(1): 35–41

Jones R (2001) Honey and healing through the ages. In: Munn P, Jones R, eds. *Honey and Healing*. IBRA, Cardiff

Kaye ET (2000) Topical antibacterial agents. *Infect Dis Clin North Am* **14**(2): 321–39

Kelly J (2001) Addressing the problem of increased antibiotic resistance. *Prof Nurs* **17**(1): 56–9

Kingsley A (2001) A proactive approach to wound infection. *Nurs Standard* **15**(30): 50–8

Klasen HJ (2000) Historical review of the use of silver in the treatment of burns. *Burns* **26**: 117–30

Kramer SA (1999) Effect of povidone-iodine on wound healing: a review. *J Vasc Nurs* **XVII**(1): 17–23

Kunisada T, Yamada K, Oda S, Hara O (1997) Investigation on the efficiency of povidone-iodine against antiseptic resistant species. *Dermatology* **195** (suppl 2) 14–18

Lanker Klossner B, Widmer H-R, Frey F (1997) Non-development of resistance by bacteria during hospital use of povidone-iodine. *Dermatology* **195** (suppl 2): 10–13

Lawrence JC (1998a) The use of iodine as an antiseptic agent. *J Wound Care* **7**(8): 421–5

Lawrence JC (1998b) A povidone-iodine medicated dressing. *J Wound Care* **7**(7): 332–6

Leak K (2002) PEG site infections: a novel use for Actisorb Silver 220. *Br J Community Nurs* **7**(6):

Leaper DJ (1988) Antiseptic toxicity in open wounds. *Nurs Times* **84**(25): 77–9

Levy S (1998) The challenge of antibiotic resistance. *Sci Am* **278**(3): 32–9

Mandell GL, Sande MA (1990) Antimicrobials. In: Goodman-Gilman A, Rall TW, Nies AS *et al*, eds. *Goodman and Gilman's The Pharmacological Basis of Therapeutics*. 8th edn. Pergamon Press, New York: 1047–64

Mangram AJ, Horan TC, Pearson ML, Silver LC, Jarvis WR (1999) Guideline for the prevention of surgical site infection, 1999. Centers for Disease Control and Prevention (CDC) Hospital Infection Control Practices Advisory Committee. *Am J Infect Control* **27**(2): 97–132

McDonnell G, Russell AD (1999) Antiseptics and disinfectants: activity, action and resistance. *Clin Microbiol Rev* **12**(1): 147–79

McLure AR, Gordon J (1992) *In vitro* evaluation of povidone-iodine and chlorhexidine against methicillin-resistant *Staphylococcus aureus. J Hosp Infect* **21**: 291–9

Mertz PM, Oliviera-Gandia MF, Davis S (1999) The evaluation of a cadexomer iodine wound dressing on methicillin resistant *Staphylococcus aureus* (MRSA) in acute wounds. *Dermatol Surg* **25**(2): 89–93

Modak SM, Fox CL (1981) Sulfadiazine silver-resistant *Pseudomonas* in burns. *Arch Surg* **116**: 854–7

Moellering RC (1995) Past, present, and future of antimicrobial agents. *Am J Med* **99**(Suppl 6A): 11S–18S

Molan PC (1992) The antibacterial activity of honey 1. The nature of the antibacterial activity. *Bee World* **73**(1): 5–28

Molan PC (1998) A brief review of the use of honey as a clinical dressing. *Primary Intention* **6**(4): 148–58

Molan PC (1999) The role of honey in the management of wounds. *J Wound Care* **8**(8): 415–8

Moore D (1992) Hypochlorites: a review of the evidence. *J Wound Care* **1**(4): 44–53

Moore K, Thomas A, Harding KG (1997) Iodine released from the wound dressing Iodosorb modulates the secretion of cytokines by human macrophages responding to bacterial lipopolysaccharide. *Int J Biochem Cell Biology* **29**(1): 163–73

Moore OA, Smith LA, Campbell F, Seers K, McQuay H (2001) Systemic review of the use of honey as a wound dressing. BMC Complementary and alternative medicine 1:2. Available online at: www.biomedcentral.com/1472-6882/1/2

Moreno F, Crisco C, Jorgensen JH, Pasttersonn JE (1995) MRSA as a community organism. *Clin Infect Dis* **21**: 1308–12

Morgan M, Evans-Williams D, Salmon R, Hosein I, Looker DN, Howard A (2000) The population impact of MRSA: the national survey of MRSA in Wales 1997. *J Hosp Infect* **44**(3): 227–39

Morison M (1990) Wound cleansing: which solution? *Nurs Standard* **4**(52): 4–6

Mycock B (1985) Methicillin antiseptic-resistant *Staphylococcus aureus. Lancet* **ii**: 949–50

Natarajan S, Williamson D, Grey J, Harding KG, Cooper RA (2001) Healing of an MRSA-colonised, hydroxyurea-induced leg ulcer with honey. *J Dermatol Treatment* **12**: 33–6

Nichols RL (1998) Post-operative infections in the age of drug-resistant Gram-positive bacteria. *Am J Med* **104**(5A): 11S–16S

O'Meara SO, Cullum N, Majid M, Sheldon T (2000) Systematic reviews of wound care management: (3) Antimicrobial agents. *Health Technol Assess* **4**(21): 1–237

O'Meara SO, Cullum N, Majid M, Sheldon T (2001) Systematic review of antimicrobial agents used for chronic wounds. *Br J Surg* **88**: 4–21

Payne DN, Babb JR, Bradley CR (1999) An evaluation of the suitability of the European suspension test to reflect *in vitro* activity of antiseptics against clinically significant organisms. *Letters in Applied Microbiology* **28**: 7–12

Pruitt BA (1987) Opportunistic infection in burn patients: diagnosis and treatment. In: Root R, Trunkey R, Sande MA, eds. *New Surgical and Medical Approaches to Infectious Diseases*. Churchill Livingstone, New York: 245–61

Rice TT (1992) Metronidazole use in malodorous skin lesions. *J Rehab Nurs* **17**(5): 244–55

Rikimaru T, Kondo M, Kajimura K, Hashimoto K, Oyamada K, Miyazak S, Sagawa K, Alzawa H, Oizumi K (2002) Efficacy of common antiseptics against multi-drug resistant *Mycobacterium tuberculosis*. *Int J Tuberculosis and Lung Diseases* **6**(9): 763–70

Rodeheaver G (1990) Controversies in topical wound management: wound cleansing and wound disinfection. In: Krasner D, ed. *Chronic Wound Care*. Pennsylvania Health Management Publications, Pennsylvania USA

Roe BH, Luker KA, Cullum NA, Griffiths JM, Kenrick M (1994) Nursing treatment of patients with chronic leg ulcers in the community: report of a survey. *J Clin Nurs* **3**(3): 159–68

Russell AD, Hugo WB (1994) Antimicrobial activity and action of silver. *Prog Med Chem* **31**: 351–70

Saffle JR, Schnebly WA (1994) Burn wound care. In: Richard RL, Stanley MJ, eds. *Burn Care and Rehabilitation: Principles and Practice*. Davis Co, Philadelphia, USA: 137–9

Scanlon E, Dowsett C (2001) Clinical governance in the control of wound infection and odour. *Br J Nurs* (Silver Suppl part 2): 9–18

Scott Ward R, Saffle JR (1995) Topical agents in burn wound care. *Phys Ther* **75**(6): 526–38

Suller MT, Russell AD (2000) Triclosan and antibiotic resistance in *Staphylococcus aureus*. *J Antimicrob Chemother* **46**(1): 11–8

SIGN (1998) Scottish intercollegiate guidelines network; The Care of Patients with Chronic Leg Ulcer. A National Clinical Guideline. Royal College of Physicians, Edinburgh. http://www.show.cee.hw.ac.uk/sign/home.htm

Sundberg J, Meller R (1997) A retrospective review of the use of cadexomer iodine in the treatment of chronic wounds. *Wounds* **9**(3): 68–86

Thomas C (1988) Nursing alert: wound healing halted with the use of povidone-iodine. *Ostomy Wound Manage* **18**(Spring): 30–3

Tonks A, Cooper RA, Price AJ, Molan PC, Jones KP (2001) Stimulation of TNFα release in monocytes by honey. *Cytokine* **14**: 240–42

Tonks A, Cooper RA, Jones KP *et al* (2003) Honey stimulates inflammatory cytokine production from monocytes. *Cytokine* in press

Traoré O, Fournet Fayard S, Laveran H (1996) An *in-vitro* evaluation of the activity of povidone-iodine against nosocomial bacterial strains. *J Hosp Infec* **34**: 217–22

White RJ (2001) An historical overview of the use of silver in wound management. *Br J Nurs* (Silver Suppl 1): 3–9

White RJ, Cooper R, Kingsley A (2001) Wound colonization and infection: the role of topical antimicrobials. *Br J Nurs* **10**(9): 563–78

White RJ, Cooper R, Kingsley A (2002) A topical issue: the use of antibacterials in wound pathogen control. In: White R, ed. *Trends in Wound Care*. Quay Books, MA Healthcare Limited, Salisbury

Williams C (1994) Actisorb Plus in the treatment of exuding infected wounds. *Br J Nurs* **3**(15): 786–8

Williams C (1997) Arglaes controlled release dressing in the control of bacteria. *Br J Nurs* **6**(2): 114–5

Willix D, Molan P, Harfoot C (1992) A comparison of the sensitivity of wound-infecting species of bacteria to the antibacterial activity of manuka honey and other honey. *J Appl Bact* **73**: 388–94

Wright JB, Lam K, Burrell RE (1998) Wound management in an era of increasing bacterial antibiotic resistance: A role for topical silver treatment. *Am J Infect Control* **26**(6): 572–7

Wright JB, Lam K, Hansen DL, Burrell RE (1999) Efficacy of topical silver against fungal burn wound pathogens. *Am J Infect Control* **27**(4): 344–50

Yin HQ, Langford R, Burrell RE (1999) Comparative evaluation of Acticoat antimicrobial barrier dressing. *J Burn Care Rehab* **20**: 195–200

Zaki I, Shall L, Dalziel KL (1994) Bacitracin: a significant sensitiser in leg ulcer patients? *Contact Dermatitis* **31**: 92–4

Zhou LH, Mahm WK, Badiavaf E, Yufit T, Fallanga V (2002) Slow release iodine preparation and wound healing: *in vitro* effects consistent with lack of *in vivo* toxicity in human chronic wounds. *Br J Dermatol* **146**: 365–74

# 7

# An historical overview of the use of silver in wound management

*Richard J White*

While silver and its compounds have been medically used for thousands of years, the recent research focus on this element has led to a resurgence in interest, particularly in the field of wound care product development. The increasing problems of antibiotic resistance, combined with concerns over the safety and toxicity of topical antiseptics, has highlighted the need for a safe agent which can be used to treat colonized and infected wounds effectively. Wounds, notably chronic wounds, can support a wide variety of micro-organisms, many of which are pathogens, and act as a source for cross-infection. While systemic antibiotics are justifiably recognized as the first-line treatment of choice for chronic wounds with spreading cellulitis and infected wounds in 'at risk' patients, not all infected wounds merit this treatment. There is now a rationale for the judicious use of suitable topical antisepsis in certain colonized, critically colonized, and infected wounds. The increasing evidence available on products containing silver suggests that this element can fulfil a valuable role in wound care. This review of the history of silver as an antibacterial covers the mode of action of preparations containing silver and concludes with a focus on silver as a component of the modern wound management products: Arglaes, Acticoat, Actisorb Silver 220 and Avance.

Man has been aware of the medicinal and preservative properties of silver for over 2000 years. The ancient Greek and Roman civilizations are credited with the use of silver vessels to keep drinking water drinkable. The addition of silver coins to containers of drinking water has continued to this day — the water tanks on spacecraft are lined with silver.

The internal, or systemic use of silver certainly dates back to the work of Angelus Sola in the early seventeenth century (Gettler *et al*, 1927). He used silver nitrate to treat epilepsy, tabes and chorea. However, this practice ceased by the beginning of the twentieth century.

## Antimicrobial properties of silver and silver compounds

The antimicrobial or germicidal property of silver and its compounds has been the basis of its medicinal use since the nineteenth century. The chemical forms used have been salts, such as silver nitrate, as well as elemental and colloidal silver. MacLeod (1912) refers to his experience with colloidal silver — Collosol Argentum — introduced by Crookes Chemists in 1911 for the treatment of bacterial infections by topical, intravenous, hypodermic and oral dosage.

The topical dosing was for impetigo, acne, septic leg ulcers and ringworm. The interest in this preparation resulted in detailed research on its bactericidal action (Marshall and Killoh, 1915). The studies used commercial Collosol (a colloidal solution of silver) at one part in 2000 silver colloid, neat and diluted, on cultures of various pathogenic bacteria *in vitro*. The time and dilution required to kill the organisms were noted. Organisms killed successfully included *Escherichia coli*, *Salmonella paratyphi A* and *B*, *Bacillus anthracis* and *Yersinia pestis*.

The major silver preparations that have seen widespread clinical use this past century are the solution of silver nitrate, silver sulphadiazine (SSD) cream and a variety of dressings containing elemental or ionized silver. There have been some other products, such as silver-zinc-allantoinate (Margraf and Covey, 1977).

The use of different topical silver preparations is closely related to wound categories, eg. SSD in burns. Without doubt, the single most studied aspect has been in burns therapy. This approach was probably first undertaken by Moyer *et al* (1965) using silver nitrate 0.5% solution. Clinical experience showed that the silver was rapidly deactivated and, to maintain efficacy, large quantities of dressings soaked in this solution had to be applied regularly to the burned area (Fox, 1983).

It is probable that, at the same time as Moyer *et al* (1965) were conducting their research, Fox (1983) was developing a compound of silver with an antibiotic, thus providing a double therapy. The antibiotics chosen for *in vitro* evaluation and *in vivo* animal model testing were penicillin and the sulphonamide sulphadiazine among others. While all were effective *in vitro*, only the sulphadiazine was effective topically in ointment formulation, particularly against pseudomonads. In addition, the sulphadiazine had the advantages of remaining white (where many other silver compounds oxidize to an unsightly black oxide) and was not deactivated by components of wound exudate. This was to become the silver sulphadiazine that is widely used today.

References to the use of silver on chronic wounds date back to studies on ulcers in the seventeenth and eighteenth centuries (Klasen, 2000a). According to Klasen (2000a), one of the earliest texts to mention silver nitrate was by John Woodall in 1617, where silver nitrate is referred to as either 'infernal stone' or 'lunar caustic'. It was regarded as an essential component of every surgeon's equipment and was used to treat venereal buboes and chancre, to open abscesses, and 'reduce proud flesh and sores'. In this context, the term 'proud flesh' refers to hypergranulation, a feature commonly seen in healing leg ulcers.

Later, in order to assist in application, silver nitrate was made into pencils. In all of these applications and formulations it is impossible to know the exact concentration used; it is highly likely that strong (10%+) preparations were used for their caustic effect rather than a subtle antibacterial effect.

The use of silver nitrate on burns and in ophthalmology appears to have begun in earnest in the early nineteenth century. We know from Klasen (2000a) that in 1830 Rust used a dilute solution (0.2%) successfully on third-degree burns. This led to widespread use, first in Germany, then later throughout Europe. Concentrations of the solution ranged from 0.2%–2.5%, with the weaker solutions being reserved for children.

It was at this time that interest in the causes for infection and antisepsis originated. The innovative works of Lister and Semmelweiss in the latter half of the nineteenth century focused attention on the link between microorganism and sepsis, and on the need for antiseptic precautions (Lawrence and Payne, 1984). The German obstetrician Crede began using 2% silver nitrate solution for gonococcal ophthalmia neonatorum from 1880. This led to successful clinical resolution of the problem and to his writing a monograph, *Silver Salts as Antiseptics* in 1896 (Klasen, 2000a).

In America, the surgeon Halstead began using silver wire sutures and silver foil dressings to reduce postoperative sepsis (Halstead, 1895). Silver nitrate solutions continued in use throughout the two great wars for the treatment of burns and sepsis. With the advent of the antibiotics, penicillin and sulphonamides, interest in silver declined.

Renewed interest, stimulated by the American surgeon Moyer, began in the 1960s (Klasen, 2000b). Infection of burns remained a serious problem despite antibiotic use, so Moyer returned to solutions of silver nitrate applied on to thick cotton gauze dressings on both burns and grafted areas (Moyer *et al*, 1965). He found that this approach was effective against *Staphylococcus aureus*, *Pseudomonas aeruginosa* and haemolytic streptococci without the development of resistance.

At the same time, silver sulphadiazine was being formulated from silver nitrate and sodium sulphadiazine in order to combine the antibacterial effect of the sulphonamide moiety with the inhibitory effect of silver (Fox, 1983). The hydrophilic cream formulation, sold as Flamazine (Smith & Nephew Healthcare) in the UK, and Silvadene in the USA, became the most widely used topical antibacterial used in burns treatment (Fakhry *et al*, 1995).

## Antimicrobial action of topical silver

Silver has been found to be active against a wide range of bacterial (Hoffmann, 1984; Hugo, 1992), fungal (Wright *et al*, 1999) and viral pathogens (Montes *et al*, 1986). Elemental silver will have the same mode of action whether or not it is compounded with other chemical moieties. The action of the silver can be differentiated from, for example, the sulphonamide antibiotic sulphadiazine in SSD (Lansdown *et al*, 1997).

The presentation of silver in the range of different products will also have an impact on efficacy, but not mode of action. Thus, silver may be available as a colloidal suspension, silver ions, or as elemental silver, depending on the product formulation.

Topical treatment of acute and chronic wounds is a selective approach to the prevention and treatment of infection. For any product to be effective in this respect, it must have certain chemical and physical properties.

With respect to a dressing that contains silver, it is important that the solubility of the silver is low, ie. it does not solubilize into the wound in a short time but slowly, over a period of days, to provide a sustained release and prolonged activity. In this way there will be no bolus dosing that would possibly give rise to transient high tissue blood and urine levels, thus maximizing the systemic toxicity (ie. unwanted side-effects) risks.

It is also important that there is no substantial chemical reactivity of the silver with wound exudate in order to achieve sustained antibacterial activity in the wound. The detailed pharmacology of silver, including SSD, has been detailed in reviews by Fox (1985) and by standard textbooks (Dollery, 1999). The antibacterial activity *in vitro* has been reviewed by Hamilton-Miller *et al* (1983), and the clinical efficacy has been reviewed by Hoffman (1984) and Wright *et al* (1999).

The critical factor in bactericidal action in the wound is the local concentration of drug required and the possibility of achieving this level by either systemic or topical application. If local blood supply is compromised, such as in ischaemic limbs, tissue oedema, and thermal coagulation, and in the presence of eschar and/or lipodermatosclerosis, the chances of systemic therapy achieving therapeutic concentrations is greatly reduced. Drugs dosed systemically, as opposed to those delivered topically, must separate freely from the plasma proteins to which they may bind, diffuse into the area of infection and, after reacting with amino acids, proteins and electrolytes in the wound, still maintain a bactericidal concentration.

## Mode of action of silver

The antibacterial effects of silver are usually attributed to the possible mechanisms listed in *Table 7.1* (Thurman and Gerba, 1989). Details of these mechanisms have been published in an extensive review by Russell and Hugo (1994).

There is evidence that wounds treated with silver nitrate and SSD heal rapidly (Margraf and Covey, 1977; Kjolseth *et al*, 1994); however, there are some contradictions (Stern, 1989).

In order to clarify the effects of silver on wound healing, Lansdown *et al* (1997) compared silver nitrate and SSD on intact and wounded rat skin. He found that both agents enhanced wound healing, possibly by the local enhancement of key trace elements zinc and calcium. This, it is postulated, is attributable to the preferential binding of silver to metallothionine, releasing zinc for metabolic functions and the formation of metalloenzymes. While this work has not been reproduced in human wounds, the evidence suggests that silver has both bactericidal and healing benefits when dosed at appropriate levels.

| Table 7.1: Possible reasons for the antibacterial effects of silver |
| --- |
| Interference with bacterial electron transport |
| Binding to DNA of bacteria and their spores thus increasing the stability of the double helix and impairing cell replication |
| Cell membrane interactions. Binding causing structural and receptor function damage |
| Formation of insoluble, and by implication, metabolically ineffective, compounds with anions, sulphydryl groups as in methionine and thiolated nucleotides, histidine and enzymes |

Source: Thurman and Gerba, 1989

## Safety and toxicity

Silver compounds may react with environmental pollutants to form the black silver sulphide. When this occurs to topical or systemically applied silver medicaments the result is a grey discolouration (argyria) of the skin, sclerae, nails and mucous membranes (Gettler *et al*, 1927; Buckley, 1963; Pariser, 1968; Lansdown, 1995). This is particularly evident after prolonged topical and systemic use of silver nitrate (Marshall and Schneider, 1977) but rarely after SSD application (Dupuis *et al*, 1985). There are no reports of argyria after the use of any of the modern wound dressings mentioned later in this chapter.

In a review of 650 cases of children treated with topical SSD 1% for burns and scalds over a five-year period, Lockhart *et al* (1983) found four instances of neutropenia and two of erythema multiforme rash. All were attributed to the sulphadiazine moiety. Urinalysis showed a mean urinary concentration of sulphadiazine of 31.8mg/l. This reflects the absorption of the active through the treated skin area and is testimony to the apparent lack of observed toxicity to silver (Boosalis *et al*, 1987). In a similar study on forty-five severely burned patients, Kulick *et al* (1985) found evidence of sulphadiazine sensitization in the form of circulating IgG antibodies. There was no reference made to toxicity to silver although any evidence of systemic and cutaneous silver toxicity was sought.

Kernicterus has been associated with the topical use of SSD, which is also attributable to the sulphonamide. Accordingly, SSD should be avoided during pregnancy, on premature infants or those under two months of age (Ward and Saffle, 1995).

Silver nitrate topical and systemic dosage forms have given rise to toxicity to the intestine (Monafo and Moyer, 1968) and to new skin cells (Demling and DiSanti, 2001). This toxicity has been attributed to the nitrate moiety, which is a potent oxidizing agent, and not to the silver.

# Formulations and compounds of silver

### Silver protein (argyrol) or mild silver protein

This is a mixture of silver nitrate, sodium hydroxide (an alkali) and gelatin for internal use. Such products are promoted as essential mineral supplements, and for the treatment of such diverse diseases as cancer, diabetes, AIDS and herpes (Fung and Bowen, 1996), although there is no theoretical or practical justification for their use (Osol and Farrar, 1960; Food and Drug Administration [FDA], 1995).

### Silver zinc allantoinate

Also known as AZAC cream, this is the combination of an antibacterial (silver), a factor in wound healing (zinc) and allantoin, an agent that stimulates debridement and tissue growth (Margraf and Covey, 1977). In a clinical trial on patients with chronic wounds, 339 out of 400 (85%) wounds healed with AZAC 1% treatment (Margraf and Covey, 1977). However, despite this promising preliminary data no further trials have been published and no product containing AZAC has found its way into routine clinical use.

### Silver sulphadiazine

This was first formulated as an ointment and an aqueous cream in 1967 (Fox, 1983). Although primarily intended for the treatment of burns, SSD has been used successfully in the treatment of leg ulcers (Margraf and Covey, 1977; Blair *et al*, 1988; Wunderlich and Orfanos, 1991; Bishop *et al*, 1992) and fingertip injuries (Buckley *et al*, 2000). In a recent systematic review of antimicrobial agents for chronic wounds, evidence was found supporting the use of SSD as a topical antimicrobial in the management of infected wounds (O'Meara *et al*, 2001).

# Recent silver-based wound dressings

Most recently, the interest in wound care, combined with concerns regarding sensitivity and resistance to topical antibiotics, has focused attention on to topical antiseptic and antibacterial agents (White *et al*, 2001). The requirements for a formulation that would provide a sustained release of a non-toxic agent has led to the development of numerous dressings containing silver.

A number of wound dressing products containing silver have been developed in the last decade. These are intended for use on colonized or infected wounds or as a prophylactic measure in at-risk patients. The rationale behind these products is: first, the need for a safe and effective topical antibacterial that provides a sustained effect over days; second, as resistance is such a problem with current antibiotics, the antibacterial should have a low or zero potential to select for resistant strains. The characteristics of the ideal silver-containing dressing are listed in *Table 7.2*.

| Table 7.2: Characteristics of the ideal silver dressing |
| --- |
| Deliver silver in a sustained therapeutic way, ie. effective antibacterial dose with limited opportunity for systemic absorption |
| Combined antimicrobial effect and capacity to absorb exudate even under high compression |
| Have an odour-control function |
| Be easy to use and comfortable for the patient |
| Be cost-effective |

Arglaes is manufactured by Maersk Medical. This transparent film, marketed in the UK since 1996, contains 10% w/w silver polymer which releases ions at a constant rate (Williams, 1997).

Silver-coated cloth (Acticoat, manufactured by Smith & Nephew Healthcare) is a high density polyethylene dressing coated with nanocrystalline silver. It has been evaluated *in vitro* and found to be effective against a variety of clinical isolates. In a comparative study in patients with burns, Acticoat was found to be more effective than silver nitrate and SSD *in vitro* (Yin *et al*, 1999) and clinically superior to silver nitrate 0.5% solution in respect of reduced wound sepsis and secondary bacteraemia (Tredget *et al*, 1998). It is also claimed to be unaffected in mode of action by the presence of proteins in wound exudate (Wright *et al*, 1998).

Actisorb Silver 220 (manufactured by Johnson & Johnson Medical), originally known as Actisorb Plus, is a combination of activated charcoal cloth impregnated with silver and enclosed within a porous nylon sleeve (Williams, 1994). The dressing adsorbs bacteria on to the charcoal cloth where they are exposed to the antibacterial activity of the silver (Furr *et al*, 1994). When compared with a charcoal cloth dressing and a chlorhexidine dressing in patients with leg ulcers, Actisorb Silver 220 was found to be the most effective for odour control, reduced frequency of dressing changes and overall improvement in ulcer condition (Millward, 1991).

Actisorb Silver 220 has also been found to be effective in venous leg ulcers (Wunderlich and Orfanos, 1991). The combination of a large surface area of odour-absorbent charcoal and bound elemental silver antiseptic is non-toxic and stimulates wound healing (Furr *et al*, 1994; Lansdown *et al*, 1997).

Silver has also been incorporated into a hydrophilic polyurethane foam dressing (Avance and Avance A adhesive, manufactured by SSL International UK). This dressing is intended for exuding wounds such as leg ulcers and pressure ulcers to help prevent cross- and self-infection. There is, however, no clinical data at the time of writing to substantiate its effectiveness.

## Conclusion

The history of the use of silver and its compounds covers the last two millennia. The value of silver as an antibacterial has not, however, been fully understood or exploited clinically until relatively recently. Evidence suggests strongly that the true value of silver is as a topical antibacterial for the prophylaxis and treatment of wound infections and in infection control.

The bacterial colonization and infection of wounds can be treated topically, systemically, or a combination of both (White *et al*, 2001). Prophylactic treatment also involves the same principles. The advantages of topical therapy are listed in *Table 7.3*.

| Table 7.3: Advantages of topical therapy |
|---|
| Only the wound and immediate tissues are exposed to the active agent rather than the whole body (as is the case with systemic treatment) |
| Higher levels of antibacterial agent are achieved in the infected wound with topical treatment |
| Reduced exposure limits toxicity and tissue reaction |
| Can be multifunctional, ie. manage odour and exudate as well as infection |

There is substantial evidence that silver and its compounds can achieve these functions, although much of this evidence currently relates to SSD in cream formulation. The recent development of alternative dressings and delivery systems shows considerable promise for antibacterial activity, and particularly the adjunctive performance features of wound deodorization (where charcoal/carbon is included) and exudate control (where an absorptive component is included).There is considerable evidence that topical silver, as the metal and colloidal forms, and in SSD formulation, is very safe.

## Key points

❖ Silver has a long history of medical use, notably in the treatment of wounds.

❖ Elemental silver, its salts, and ionic form are antiseptics active against a wide range of microorganisms, including bacteria and fungi.

❖ Topical silver preparations, particularly silver sulphadiazine, have been widely used in burns therapy and are of proven efficacy. The successful use of silver sulphadiazine on infected chronic wounds and acute, traumatic wounds has also been demonstrated.

❖ The application of silver-based dressings for wound care is relatively recent. These have a role to play in treating localized infection and in infection control.

❖ More clinical evidence, from controlled trials, is required in order to define better the uses and value of silver-containing dressings in wound management and infection control.

# References

Bishop JB, Phillips LG, Mustoe TA *et al* (1992) A prospective randomized evaluator-blinded trial of two potential wound healing agents for the treatment of venous stasis ulcers. *J Vasc Surg* **16**: 251–7

Blair SD, Backhouse CM, Wright DD *et al* (1988) Do dressings influence the healing of chronic venous ulcers? *Phlebology* **3**: 129–34

Boosalis MG, McCall JT, Arenholtz DH, Solem LD (1987) Serum and urinary silver levels in thermal injury patients. *Surgery* **101**: 40–3

Buckley WR (1963) Localized argyria. *Arch Dermatol* **88**: 531–9

Buckley SC, Scott S, Das K (2000) Late review of the use of silver sulphadiazine dressings for the treatment of fingertip injuries. *Injury* **31**: 301–4

Demling RH, DiSanti L (2001) The role of silver technology in wound healing. *Wounds* **13**(1): A 5–A15

Dollery C (1999) *Therapeutic Drugs*. 2nd edn. Churchill Livingstone, London

Dupuis LL, Shear NH, Zucker RM (1985) Hyperpigmentation due to topical application of silver sulfadiazine cream. *J Am Acad Dermatol* **12**(6): 1112–14

Fakhry SM, Alexander J, Smith D (1995) Regional and institutional variations in burn care. *J Burn Care Rehabil* **16**: 86–90

FDA (1995) *Health Fraud Bulletin No 19 and Promotional Materials from Manufacturers of Products*. Non-traditional Drug Compliance Branch, Center for Drug Evaluation and Research, FDA, Rockville, Maryland

Fox CL (1983) Topical therapy and the development of silver sulfadiazine. *Surg Oncol Obstet* **157**(1): 82–8

Fox CL (1985) The human pharmacology of silver sulphadiazine. *J Burns Inc Therm Injury* **11**(4): 306–7

Fung MC, Bowen DL (1996) Silver products for medical indications: risk-benefit assessment. *Clin Toxicol* **34**(1): 119–26

Furr JR, Russell AD, Turner TD, Andrews A (1994) Antibacterial activity of Actisorb Plus, Actisorb and silver nitrate. *J Hosp Infect* **27**: 201–8

Gettler AO, Rhoads CP, Weiss S (1927) A contribution to the pathology of generalized argyria with a discussion on the fate of silver in the human body. *Am J Pathol* **3**: 631–51

Hamilton-Miller JM, Shah S, Smith C (1983) Silver sulphadiazine: a comprehensive *in vitro* assessment. *Chemotherapy* **39**: 405–9

Halstead WS (1895) The operative treatment of hernia. *Am J Med Sci* **110**: 13–17

Hoffmann S (1984) Silver sulfadiazine: an antibacterial agent for topical use in burns. *Scand J Plast Reconstr Surg* **18**: 119–26

Hugo WB (1992) In: Russell AD, Hugo WB, Ayliffe GAJ, eds. *Principles and Practice of Disinfection, Preservation and Sterilization*. 2nd edn. Blackwell Scientific, Oxford: 3–6

Klasen HJ (2000a) Historical review of the use of silver in the treatment of burns. Early uses. *Burns* **26**: 117–30

Klasen HJ (2000b) A historical review of the use of silver in the treatment of burns. Renewed interest for silver. *Burns* **26**: 131–8

Kjolseth D, Frank JM, Barker JH *et al* (1994) Comparison of the effects of commonly-used wound agents on epithelialization and neovascularization. *J Am Coll Surg* **179**: 305–12

Kulick MI, Wong R, Okarma TB, Falces E, Berkowitz RL (1985) Prospective study of side- effects associated with the use of silver sulfadiazine in severely burned patients. *Ann Plast Surg* **14**(5): 407–18

Lansdown ABG (1995) Physiological and toxicological changes in the skin resulting from the action and interaction of metal ions. *Crit Rev Toxicol* **25**(5): 397–462

Lansdown ABG, Sampson B, Laupattaraksem P *et al* (1997) Silver aids healing in the sterile skin wound: experimental studies in the laboratory rat. *Br J Dermatol* **137**: 728–35

Lawrence JC, Payne MJ (1984) *Wound Healing*. The Update Group, London: 15–20

Lockhart SP, Rushworth A, Azmy AAF, Raine PA (1983) Topical silver sulphadiazine: side-effects and urinary excretion. *Burns* **10**: 9–12

MacLeod CEA (1912) Electric metallic colloids and their therapeutical applications. *Lancet* 3 February: 322–3

Margraf HW, Covey TH (1977) A trial of silver-zinc-allantoinate in the treatment of leg ulcers. *Arch Surg* **112**: 699–704

Marshall CR, Killoh GB (1915) The bactericidal action of collosols of silver and mercury. *Br Med J* **16** January: 102–4

Marshall JP, Schneider RP (1977) Systemic argyria secondary to topical silver nitrate. *Arch Dermatol* **113**: 1077–9

Millward P (1991) Comparing treatment for leg ulcers. *Nurs Times* **87**(13): 70–2

Monafo W, Moyer C (1968) The treatment of extensive thermal burns with 0.5% silver nitrate solution. *Ann NY Acad Sci* **150**: 937–45

Montes LF, Muchinik G, Fox CL (1986) Response to varicella-zoster virus and herpes zoster to silver sulfadiazine. *Cutis* **38**(6): 363–5

Moyer C, Brentano L, Gravens DL, Margraf HW, Monafo WW (1965) Treatment of large human burns with 0.5% silver nitrate solution. *Arch Surg* **90**: 812–67

O'Meara SM, Cullum NA, Majid M, Sheldon TA (2001) Systematic review of antimicrobial agents used for chronic wounds. *Br J Surg* **88**: 4–21

Osol A, Farrar GE (1960) *The Dispensary of the United States of America*. 25th edn. Lippincott, Philadelphia: 1233–9

Pariser RJ (1968) Generalized argyria. *Arch Dermatol* **114**: 373–7

Russell AD, Hugo WB (1994) Antimicrobial activity and action of silver. *Prog Med Chem* **31**: 351–70

Stern HS (1989) Silver sulphadiazine and the healing of partial-thickness burns: a prospective clinical trial. *Br J Plast Surg* **42**: 581–5

Thurman RB, Gerba CP (1989) The molecular mechanisms of copper and silver ion disinfection of bacteria and viruses. *CRC Critical Reviews in Environmental Control* **18**(4): 295–15

Tredget EE, Shankowsky HA, Groenvald A, Burrell R (1998) A matched-pair, randomized study evaluating the efficacy and safety of Acticoat silver-coated dressing for the treatment of burn wounds. *J Burn Care Rehabil* **19**(6): 531–7

Ward RS, Saffle JR (1995) Topical agents in burn and wound care. *Phys Ther* **75**(6): 526–38

White RJ, Cooper R, Kingsley A (2001) Wound colonization and infection: the role of topical antiseptics. *Br J Nurs* **10**(9): 563–78

Williams C (1994) Actisorb Plus in the treatment of exuding infected wounds. *Br J Nurs* **3**(15): 786–8

Williams C (1997) Arglaes controlled release dressing in the control of bacteria. *Br J Nurs* **6**(2): 114–15

Wright JB, Lam K, Burrell RE (1998) Wound management in an era of increasing bacterial antibiotic resistance: a role for topical silver treatment. *Am J Infect Control* **26**(6): 572–7

Wright JB, Lam K, Hansen D, Burrell RE (1999) Efficacy of topical silver against fungal burn wound pathogens. *Am J Infect Control* **27**(4): 344–50

Wunderlich U, Orfanos CE (1991) Behandlung der ulcera cruris venosa mit trockenen Wundauflagen. Phasenubergreifende Anwendung eines silber-impragnierten Aktivkohle-Xerodressings. *Hautarzt* **42**: 446–50

Yin HQ, Langford R, Burrell RE (1999) Comparative evaluation of the antimicrobial activity of Acticoat antimicrobial barrier dressing. *J Burn Care Rehabil* **20**(3): 195–200

# 8

# Clinical governance in the control of wound infection and odour

*Liz Scanlon, Caroline Dowsett*

This chapter explores the use of silver in the management of wound infection and odour from a clinical governance perspective. It relates issues of risk assessment and management, clinical effectiveness and evidence-based care, clinical audit and quality assurance to the care of patients with or at risk of a wound infection. A case study is included on the use of Actisorb Silver 220 in the management of a leg ulcer patient.

The White Paper *The New NHS: Modern, Dependable* (Department of Health [DoH], 1997), marked a fundamental and significant shift towards involving clinicians in the assurance of quality and accountability in healthcare delivery. The paper stated:

*The Government will require every NHS Trust to embrace the concept of clinical governance, so that quality is at the core, both of their responsibilities as organizations and of each of their staff as individual professionals.*

In *A First Class Service: Quality in the New NHS* (DoH, 1998) clinical governance is defined as:

*... a framework through which all NHS organizations are accountable for continuously improving the quality of their services and safeguarding high standards of care by creating an environment in which excellence in clinical care will flourish.*

The principles of clinical governance apply to all those who provide or manage patient care services in the NHS. Clinical governance incorporates a number of processes, including:

- clinical effectiveness
- clinical risk management
- clinical audit
- quality assurance and performance management
- education, training and continuing professional development.

This chapter illustrates the direct impact of these principals on wound management, and on the management of infected and malodorous wounds in particular.

# Wound infection

The presence of microorganisms in a wound is not unusual, but not all wounds support the same range and number of species (Cooper and Lawrence, 1996). Chronic wounds in particular, eg. leg ulcers and pressure ulcers, are usually colonized with a mixture of species, many of which can be potential pathogens. Dow *et al* (1999) and Kingsley (2001) proposed the notion of a wound infection continuum ranging from sterility to infection (*Table 8.1*).

| Table 8.1: The infection continuum | | | | |
|---|---|---|---|---|
| **Increasing severity** ————————————————————————➤ | | | | |
| **Sterility** | **Contamination** | **Colonization** | **Critical colonization** | **Infection** |
| Acute wounds | Acute wounds | Acute and chronic wounds | Acute and chronic wounds | Acute and chronic wounds |
| Absence of microbes | Presence of microbes but little active growth | Balanced growth and death of microbes | Host defences unable to maintain health balance | Host defences overwhelmed, local spread of cellulitis (may lead to bacteraemia, septicaemia and death) |
| Very brief period following initial surgical incision or thermal trauma | Present soon after wounding, progresses quickly to colonization | Situation normal | Delay in healing | Exacerbation of wound |
| **No action** | **Action** | **Action** | **Action** | **Action** |
| Situation will not persist in wound healing by secondary infection | No need to artificially prevent colonization. Wound healing by secondary intention (with the possible exception of burns) | Do not disturb balance (with the possible exception of diabetic foot ulcers) | Consider using antiseptic dressings to return wound to colonization | Systemic antibiotics ± antiseptic dressings |

Source: Kingsley, 2001

The development of a wound infection can have a considerable impact on a patient's quality of life, causing pain and anxiety; in some cases it can be life-threatening. It is costly in terms of treatment and prolonged hospitalization. In the wound itself, infection:

- delays wound healing
- prolongs the inflammatory phase of healing
- disrupts the normal clotting mechanism
- depletes the components of the 'complement cascade'
- disorders leukocyte function
- causes less efficient angiogenesis and formation of granulation tissue (Robson, 1990).

It is essential that the correct diagnosis of a wound infection be made before commencing any treatments. Diagnosis of an infection is best made through a full assessment, identification of clinical signs and symptoms associated with infection and laboratory tests. Criteria used to identify infection are in practice often restricted to the presence of pus, or pus with inflammation, but these criteria are not very useful when assessing chronic wounds for infection. Cutting and Harding (1994) suggested a list of additional criteria to assist the practitioner in the identification of infection in a wound (*Table 8.2*). If the additional criteria only are present this may be an indication of critical colonization which could be managed with topical antiseptics (White *et al*, 2001).

Where signs and symptoms of infection have been identified a wound swab or tissue sample may be taken for analysis of the pathogens involved. While micro-biological studies cannot conclusively identify the organism causing an infection, the more information provided on the procedure request form regarding the site, the presentation and progress of the wound and any co-morbidity, the more useful the results.

| Table 8.2: Signs and symptoms of infection | |
|---|---|
| **Traditional criteria** | **Additional criteria** |
| Abscess | Delayed healing |
| Cellulitis (heat, pain, oedema and erythema) | Discolouration (usually appears dull and dark red) |
| Increased discharge — serous | Fragile tissue which bleeds easily |
| Seropurulent, haemopurulent pus | Unexpected pain or tenderness |
| | Bridging of soft tissue |
| | Pocketing at wound base |
| | Abnormal smell |
| | Wound breakdown |
| | Necrotic/sloughy tissue (not explained by pressure damage) |

## Clinical effectiveness

The fundamental principle of quality is based on the use of effective interventions. For interventions to be effective they need to be based on evidence. Evidence-based practice takes place when, 'decisions that affect the care of patients are taken with due weight according to all valid, relevant information' (Hicks, 1997). A review of the evidence on the management of infection and associated malodour will direct the practitioner to the most effective interventions. Where rigorous evidence from randomized controlled trials (RCTs) does not exist, the practitioner must appraise all other information and assess its value for their own practice.

Patients do develop wound infections, often with associated malodour. The practitioner has to fulfil a duty of care to the patient, based on the so-called Bolam principle. This states that actions must be: 'In accordance with the practice accepted as proper by a responsible body of people skilled in that particular art' (Ferguson, 1999). Practice therefore needs to be based on the most up-to-date evidence and also acceptable to the patient.

In terms of treatment, systemic antibiotics are considered essential for the treatment of clinically infected wounds (Bowler *et al*, 2001) (*Table 8.2*). However, most practitioners will be aware of the increasing problem of antibiotic resistance. Since there is a risk of not completely eradicating the bacteria from the wound, the use of topical antibiotics is not recommended for routine treatment of colonized or infected wounds (*Drug and Therapeutics Bulletin*, 1991). In addition, there are concerns over the safety and toxicity of topical antiseptics (Leaper, 1988).

As a result of these considerations, there is growing interest in compounds such as silver that can be used to treat colonization and infection in wounds, and also as a prophylactic measure in at-risk patients (White *et al*, 2001).

Silver and silver compounds have been routinely used as bactericides for over a century. Silver impairs the electron transport system and some of the DNA function of bacteria (Cervantes and Silver, 1996; Russell and Hugo, 1994). Silver has been found to be active against a wide range of bacterial (Hoffmann, 1984; Hugo 1992), fungal (Wright *et al*, 1999) and viral pathogens (Montes *et al*, 1986).

O'Meara *et al* carried out a systematic review of management of chronic wounds with antimicrobial agents in 2000 as part of the Department of Health's health technologies assessment programme. This review identified any controlled trials which showed evidence of the effectiveness of antimicrobials. The results were equivocal, although small sample sizes and flawed study design may have contributed to this.

Other studies have been carried out using silver products, the evidence from which can be used appropriately to inform practice. Details on some of this evidence can be found in *Chapter 9*.

## Clinical risk management

Clinical governance acknowledges that clinical decision-making is a risk-management process (DoH, 1998). Within the management of infected and potentially infected wounds there are many decisions that are made by weighing up the clinical risks.

Assessment of the patient's risk of developing a wound infection is an essential element of good practice. Many factors are associated with increased risk of infection in patients. They include:

- age
- obesity
- prolonged pre-operative hospital stay
- the presence of infection at another site
- severity and number of concurrent disease (Dow *et al*, 1999).

Other important factors include:

- malnutrition: obesity and a lack of vitamin C
- low serum albumin
- diabetes mellitus
- immunosuppressive therapy
- presence of dead tissue, foreign body or haematoma at the wound site (Cruse and Foord, 1980).

Strategies that aim to reduce the risks, once identified, should be part of the patient's care package, eg. improvement in diet, or control of blood glucose in a patient with diabetes.

A decision regarding whether to use a clean or aseptic technique for treating the wound will be based on a risk assessment. Inappropriate use of aseptic technique may be uncomfortable for the patient, time consuming and costly. However, failure to use aseptic technique when treating an at-risk patient could be detrimental to the patient, clinician and other patients.

A decision whether to swab a wound will be based on an assessment of the risks and benefits. The patient may find the procedure painful and be anxious about the results. The procedure is costly, and the results may not identify the causative organism. However, the risk of not treating an infection or a delay in treatment due to prescription of the wrong antibiotic must be taken into account.

Decisions over the use of topical antiseptics or systemic antibiotics will need to be taken, weighing up the risks of both interventions. As previously discussed, the use of systemic antibiotics should be preserved for infections as described in *Table 8.2*, and the use of topical antibiotics is, in most cases, thought to be inappropriate. Certain exceptions may include topical metronidazole, where the benefits (ie. a reduction in the number of anaerobic bacteria and so the management of odour) could outweigh the risks. A decision over the use of topical antiseptics needs to be based on an assessment of the risks, eg. the toxic effect on certain types of cells in healthy wounds and the potential to delay healing, compared to the benefits of reducing the bacterial load in a wound where prevention of infection or the management of odour is a priority.

Similarly, the decision of whether to use Actisorb Silver 220 (Johnson & Johnson Medical Ltd, Ascot) will also need to be based on an assessment of the risks and benefits. The benefits are described by Hampton (*Chapter 10*; 2001) and include the management of odour, reduction in exudates and reduction in bacterial load. The risks include inability to manage excessive bacterial load or odour, unnecessary costs of treatment if aims are not being achieved, or localised reactions such as pain and sensitivity.

## Clinical audit

The purpose of clinical audit is to improve the quality of care to patients locally. Audit entails measuring current practice against agreed standards of best practice, and taking appropriate action to ensure high standards are being met. Audit should measure patient outcomes and quality of care. This could be, for example, through monitoring reduction in infection and odour, healing of the wound and patient satisfaction surveys.

There are few published reports of normal wound healing rates. Specific details on healing of infected or colonized wounds or the effectiveness of odour management are even less common. Surveillance of surgical wound infection is carried out in acute care settings by infection control staff. However, the reliability of this data is being called into question as more patients are discharged early before infection is identified. Community surveillance is difficult to carry out due to the variety of different care options for each patient. Individual clinicians have a duty to contribute to local audits and set local benchmarks for practice.

## Quality assurance and performance management

Quality assurance involves regular monitoring of quality measures such as frequency and review of critical incidents, patient involvement and satisfaction, clinic waiting times and attendance. Such monitoring provides a measure of current practice and informs the development of new ways of working with the aim of improving patient care.

When critical incidents do happen, it is essential that lessons are learned in an open and blame-free culture. Reviews of incidents should occur at clinical supervision level where staff should be encouraged to reflect on their own practice, the occurrence of minor incidents and 'near miss' incidents, eg. the patient who repeatedly develops wound infections, or the person who is becoming socially isolated as a result of self-consciousness about the wound odour.

Serious incidents such as systemic infections or limb infections which lead to gangrene and amputation, should be shared with as many staff as possible as a learning exercise to identify the cause of the incident and to address practice and training issues. Where necessary, guidelines and competencies should be reviewed, both for the individuals involved and for the organization.

Patient and user involvement is an essential component of clinical governance and quality assurance. This should occur on a local level for guideline development and for individual treatment decisions. Having non-professional membership of clinical governance councils is important when developing patient services and clinical guidelines in the management of wound infection and odour. This will ensure that the patient perspective is given due weight in deciding how services are delivered.

Issues such as pain, odour control, and impact of the wound on quality of life and body image are particularly relevant to the prevention of wound infection. Patient involvement is a key to the success of any treatment plan. If the patient wishes to redress a wound themselves, then the nurse has a duty to ensure they carry out the procedure safely to minimize the risk of infection. Patient understanding of their wound is essential if optimum healing is to be achieved.

There needs to be a balance between the patient's perspective of the problem and that of the health professional. On this basis, a negotiated care package can be developed and tailored to meet individual patient's needs.

## Education, training and continuing professional development

Clinical governance relies on the theoretical knowledge base and clinical skills of practitioners. As practice changes in light of new evidence, there is a need to update staff. The management of wound infection and odour requires knowledge of:

- the differences between infection and colonization
- the risk factors for wound infection
- microbiology and the significance of different types of bacteria on wounds and in tissues
- the causes of wound odour and options for management
- the effects of systemic and topical antimicrobials on wound healing
- the long-term effects of delayed wound healing due to critical colonization and infection.

These key areas need to be part of any educational programme and from this knowledge base clinical skills should be developed. Training needs to be ongoing and responsive to new evidence and developments in wound infection and in particular the use of topical antiseptics. We know that the use of antibiotics and antiseptics for wound management continues to be controversial. It is particularly important that the nurse maintains an up-to-date knowledge of new research and current expert opinion. The nurse must also reflect carefully on each wound management decision to ensure that the care has been appropriate for that individual.

The following case study is an example of how the elements of clinical governance that have been discussed can be implemented in clinical practice for the overall benefit of the patients. The case study describes the use of Actisorb Plus in the management of venous leg ulcers. The tissue viability nurse (TVN) was familiar with the evidence related to the clinical effectiveness of the Actisorb Plus. The decision-making process for the management of this patient involved weighing up the risks, the potential for amputation and the risk of recurrent infections against the risks associated with the different treatment options.

The tissue viability nurse maintained regular contact to monitor the performance of the products and the staff. The patient was fully involved in the treatment plan and he identified odour management as a priority outcome. The assessment of the patient led to the identification of training needs for the nurses, as they were not familiar with the bandaging techniques required for limbs where the circumference was significantly increased.

# Case study of a patient with malodorous wounds

Mr S was a forty-eight-year-old man. He had been involved in a road traffic accident when he was twenty-one and had paraplegia resulting from a spinal fracture. His initial rehabilitation had enabled him to be self-caring. He used a transfer board to move between bed and chair and occasionally drove a car which had been adapted with hand controls. Mr S spent most of his time at his computer.

As a consequence of sitting in his wheelchair at his computer for most of the day and night, he had developed gravitational oedema which over time had led to some lymphoedema. Both legs had significant ulceration which had initially been caused by trauma occurring during transfers. The ulcers on his legs were being treated by district nurses who were visiting daily. Because Mr S could not feel his legs there was no pain associated with the ulcers.

The main problems were the amount of exudate from the limbs, which frequently soiled clothes or bedding and the odour from the wounds. The leg ulcers had gradually deteriorated over the years until they extended over most of the gaiter area and the foot. Mr S generally disliked hospitals, but had eventually agreed to see a vascular surgeon who had suggested amputation of the limbs. Although his legs were a problem Mr S did not wish to have them amputated. The district nurses had then referred Mr S to a tissue viability nurse.

An assessment by the tissue viability nurse identified both limbs with significant oedema, circumferential leg ulcers which were 100% sloughy and draining copious amounts of green exudate. They were being managed conservatively with polyurethane foam dressings, Gamgee tissue and crepe bandages. The odour from the wounds was noticeable in the room and offensive when the dressings were removed. There was no obvious cellulitis at the time although Mr S had had many courses of antibiotics in the past. A Doppler test was performed by the tissue viability nurse using an extra large blood pressure cuff (which had been unavailable to the district nurses), and ankle and calf measurements were taken. The ankle brachial pressure index (ABPI) for the left leg was 0.87 and the other was 0.76, indicating an adequate blood supply on the left leg and partially compromised arterial supply in the right leg. The ankle circumferences were 30 cm for the left leg and 28 cm for the right.

A management plan was agreed with Mr S. The short-term aims were to manage the exudate and odour, and tackle the colonization. Actisorb Plus (now Actisorb Silver 220) — an activated charcoal cloth impregnated with silver — was applied to the sloughy areas wherever practical. It was felt that the use of silver sulphadiazine cream might lead to an increase in maceration, and the wounds were too extensive for the use of cadexomer iodine ointment or paste.

The wounds were then covered with absorbent pads and a layer of orthopaedic wool applied. This was to offer extra absorption and to reshape the limbs in preparation for compression. Due to the amount of muscle wasting in the lower limbs from the years of inactivity, the legs had become cylindrical in shape. It was important to build up a calf shape to ensure graduated compression could be applied.

The ankle circumferences were re-measured once adequate padding had been applied (the amount of pressure from the bandage is inversely proportional to the circumference of the limb). The number and type of bandages had to be adjusted for the excessive limb size.

The left ankle now measured 35 cm, and a type 3a and a 3c bandage and a cohesive bandage were applied. Reduced compression was applied to the right leg due to the lower Doppler reading; the right ankle measured 30 cm so this was bandaged with a type 3c and a cohesive bandage. The bandages were applied to achieve appropriate levels of compression.

The wounds were redressed every day for the first week, then the staff found that the frequency of dressing changes could gradually be reduced. After eight weeks the legs were being redressed weekly. The exudates now resembled serous fluid rather than being thick, green and offensive-smelling. The odour which previously had been apparent around the whole house was much reduced, and there was only a slight odour on removal of the dressing. The slough was reduced to approximately 70% of the wound and where it was present it was noticeably thinner.

After twelve weeks there was significant reduction in wound size with areas of new epithelial tissue appearing. The proportion of sloughy tissue was reduced to 40%. There was also a clear line of demarcation where the Actisorb Silver 220 had been applied to the foot but not the toes. The foot had granulating tissue presenting where distal to the line of the edge of the Actisorb Silver 220 was still completely covered in slough. Believing that the Actisorb Silver 220 had contributed to the reduction of the slough, it was applied to the toes and folded in between them.

Four weeks later the toes had only a very thin layer of slough. At this point it was decided to discontinue the Actisorb Silver 220 as the wounds were progressing well, the slough was resolving, the odour was barely noticeable and the exudate was so reduced that only a 20 x10 cm pad was required on one ulcerated area on the left leg, and the sub-bandage wadding. The ankle circumferences were re-measured every week and as the limb reduced in size the thickness of the padding was reduced. The bandage combinations were also altered accordingly to maintain the optimum pressure at the ankle.

This treatment regime is still being maintained. The ulcers are improving slowly. The most important thing for Mr S is the reduction in exudate so that he only needs to see the district nurse once a week. He is very pleased that the odour has gone and now finds his legs less heavy to lift in and out of bed.

## Discussion

The assessment of Mr S's legs led to the identification of some short-term goals. The professionals previously involved in his care had not shown any confidence in the possibility of the legs healing. Mr S was not willing to undergo amputation. He did need an improvement in his quality of life. Treatment aims focused on the management of odour, exudate, the reduction of slough and reducing the risk of cellulitis.

The use of Actisorb Silver 220 played a significant role in meeting the goals by managing the odour and reducing the number of bacteria. The recording and reassessment of the ankle circumference led to the appropriate bandage regime being used. This, in turn, led to significant reduction in oedema and therefore contributed to the reduced exudate.

## Conclusion

Clinical governance is not a new concept; improving quality of services should be high on the agenda of all practitioners. The framework offered by clinical governance is a powerful tool that supports the practitioner in doing the right thing, at the right time, in the right way, for each individual patient. The framework of clinical governance is built around evidence-based practice leading to the delivery of effective health care. Where good RCT evidence is not available, identifying the correct intervention for patients becomes more difficult. It is therefore important that each individual practitioner maintains an interest in debates regarding best practice and is able to critique and assimilate information for themselves.

The case study does not constitute high-grade evidence but describes one clinical situation where a patient's quality of life was improved with the use of Actisorb Silver 220 as part of a management plan. Practitioners are encouraged to reflect on all the information provided here and use it appropriately as part of the evidence base for their practice. They can then be confident they are offering their patients a quality service.

## Key points

- ❖ Clinical governance is a tool for helping individuals as well as organizations improve the quality of patient care.

- ❖ The identification of infection is a complex process and requires extensive theoretical knowledge and clinical experience.

- ❖ The effects of wound infection can be costly, both to the patient in terms of their quality of life and financially to the health service.

- ❖ Treatment outcomes should be discussed and agreed with the patient. Where odour management is an issue for the patient this should be given high priority.

❖ Clinical decision making is a risk management process. The nurse should use the evidence base and weigh up the risks and benefits to the patient when implementing care.

# References

Bowler PG, Duerden BI, Armstrong DG (2001) Wound microbiology and associated approaches to wound management. *Clin Microbiol Rev* **14**(2): 244– 69

Cervantes C, Silver S (1996) Metal resistance in Pseudomonas: genes and mechanisms. In: Nakazawa T, Furakawa K, Hass D, Silver S, eds. *Molecular Biology of Pseudomonas*. American Society for Microbiology, Wasington DC

Cooper R, Lawrence JC (1996) Microorganisms and wounds. *J Wound Care* **5**(5): 233–6

Cruse P, Foord R (1980) The epidemiology of wound infection: a 10-year prospective study f 62,939 wounds. *Surg Clin North Am* **60**(1): 27–40

Cutting KF, Harding KG (1994) Criteria for identifying wound infection. *J Wound Care* **3**(4): 198–201

Department of Health (1997) *The New NHS: Modern, Dependable*. The Stationery Office, London

Department of Health (1998) *A First Class Service. Quality in the New NHS*. The Stationery Office, London

Dow G, Browne A, Sibbald GR (1999) Infection in chronic wounds: controversies in diagnosis and treatment. *Ostomy, Wound Management* **45**(8): 23–40

Drug and Therapeutics Bulletin (1991) Local application to wounds 1: Cleansers, antibacterials, debriders. *Drug Ther Bull* **29**(240): 93–5

Ferguson AL (1999) Legal implications of clinical governance. In: Lugon M, Secker-Walker J, eds. *Clinical Governance, Making it Happen*. Royal Society of Medicine Press, London

Hicks N (1997) Evidence based health care. *Bandolier* **39**. http://www.jr2.ox.ac.uk/bandolier/band39/b39-9.html (accessed 13 November 2001)

Hampton S (2001) Actisorb Silver 220: a unique antibacterial dressing. *Br J Nurs* **10**(15 Silver Supplement): 17–9

Hoffman S (1984) Silver sulfadiazine: an antibacterial agent for topical use in burns. *Scand J Plast Reconstr Surg* **18**: 119–26

Hugo WB (1992) In: Russell AD, Hugo WB, Ayliffe GA, eds. *Principles and Practice of Disinfection, Preservation and Sterilization*. 2nd edn. Blackwell Scientific, Oxford: 3–6

Kingsley A (2001) A proactive approach to wound infection. *Nurs Standard* **15**(30): 50–8

Leaper DJ (1998) Defining infection. *J Wound Care* **7**(8): 373

Montes LF, Muchinik G, Fox CL (1986) Response to varicella-zoster virus and herpes zoster to silver sulfadiazine. *Cutis* **38**(6): 363–5

O'Meara SO, Cullum NI, Majid M *et al* (2000) Systematic reviews of wound care management 3: antimicrobial agents. *Health Technol Assess* **4**(21): 1–237

Robson M(1990) Wound healing alterations caused by infection. *Clin Plast Surg* **17**(3): 485–92

Russell AD, Hugo WB (1994) Antimicrobial activity and action of silver. *Prog Med Chem* **31**: 351–70

White RJ, Cooper R, Kingsley A (2001) Wound colonization and infection: the role of topical antimicrobials. *Br J Nurs* **10**(9): 563–78

Wright JB, Lam K, Hansen DL *et al* (1999) Efficacy of topical silver against fungal burn wound pathogens. *Am J Infect Control* **27**(4): 344–50

Wunderlich U, Orfanos CE (1991) Treatment of venous ulcera cruris with dry wound dressings. Phase overlapping use of silver impregnated activated charcoal xerodressing [In German]. *Hautarzt* **42**(7): 446–50

# 9

# A charcoal dressing with silver in wound infection: clinical evidence

*Richard J White*

Silver, in elemental and compound forms, has a long and successful history as an antimicrobial. In particular, silver has been widely used in wound care, notably the treatment of burns. The relatively recent development of dressings containing silver has led to a resurgence of interest and more widespread use. In order to satisfy the need for clinical evidence on which practice may be based, this review has been compiled using published and unpublished clinical trial data on the most commonly-used silver dressing in the UK. The focus on clinical effectiveness and adverse events associated with treatment interventions in a range of chronic and acute wounds serves as a basis for guidelines on good clinical care of colonised, critically colonised, infected and malodorous wounds. Actisorb Silver 220 is, according to the available evidence from comparative and non-comparative trials involving over 12000 patients, effective in reducing wound malodour, effective in promoting wound healing, and safe.

Silver and its compounds have equivocal supporting evidence in chronic wounds (O'Meara *et al*, 2001). However, this is attributable to the relative lack of published evidence from randomised, controlled clinical trials. The history of silver in wound care and an overview of silver dressings has been recently published (*Chapter 3* [Cutting, 2001]; *Chapter 7* [White, 2001]; White *et al*, 2001). In light of the historical interest in silver and of the recent interest in silver-containing dressings, this review focuses on the most widely used silver dressing in the UK — Actisorb Silver 220 (Johnson & Johnson Medical Ltd, Ascot). This product was first marketed in the UK from 1985 as Actisorb — a charcoal cloth, made by carbonizing woven viscose rayon fabric, sealed within a nylon sleeve. This product was positioned as a treatment for malodorous wounds. In 1987 silver, as metal impregnation, was added in order to provide an antimicrobial activity to complement the deodorizing effect of the charcoal (Furr *et al*, 1994). In 2000, this product (Actisorb Plus) was renamed Actisorb Silver 220 (AS220). This is currently the leading product in terms of market share (23–25%) within the sector of the UK dressings market that includes products for the management of wound bioburden, eg. povidone-iodine and cadexomer iodine preparations, all silver-containing dressings, silver sulphadiazine cream, topical metronidazole and mupirocin, and charcoal-containing dressings.

Investigations into the microbial flora of wounds began in 1874 when Billroth detected streptococci in wounds. Since then improvements in techniques have allowed the recovery, identification and enumeration of a wide variety of microbial species. Many wounds support relatively stable, mixed communities of microorganisms, often without signs of clinical infection. Some wound inhabitants, however, are capable of causing infection. The delicate balance between wound colonization and wound infection depends on the outcome of the interplay between a multitude of complicated host and microbial influences (Emmerson, 1998). Numbers and types of microorganisms in wounds are never uniform (Cooper and Lawrence, 1996), and acute wounds may contain communities distinct from those in chronic wounds (Bowler and Davies, 1999). Despite extensive investigation into the effects of microorganisms in wounds, a consensus on their impact on the wound healing process has not yet been reached (Bowler *et al*, 2001).

During World War I, French military surgeons recognized that wounds containing high numbers of microorganisms (or low numbers of streptococci) were prone to infection and should be healed by secondary intention (Hepburn, 1919). Elek (1956) showed that introducing 7.5 x $10^6$ staphylococci into normal skin induced pustule formation and that similar effects were caused by lower bacterial numbers when skin was compromised by sutures. Teplitz *et al* (1964) studied the effect of *Pseudomonas aeruginosa* in burns created in rats, and found that $10^5$ colony forming units (cfu)/g induced invasion and systemic sepsis. Although definitions of wound infection vary (Leaper, 1998), there is sufficient evidence to demonstrate a relationship between elevated microbial numbers and wound infection (Lookingbill *et al*, 1978; Bornside and Bornside, 1979; Raahave *et al*, 1986; Breidenbach and Trager, 1995). Furthermore, failure of skin grafts in wounds with elevated bacterial populations (Teplitz *et al*, 1964; Krizek *et al*, 1967; Robson and Heggers, 1969; Robson and Heggers, 1970) has also contributed to the general acceptance that a wound bioburden of $10^5$ cfu/g or cm$^2$ indicates an infected wound (or $10^4$ cfu/g in complex extremity wounds) (Breidenbach and Trager, 1995), and that population sizes below this level are required for successful grafting.

Although several studies have indicated that infected wounds exhibit accelerated healing (Tenorio *et al*, 1976; Raju *et al*, 1977), most studies have shown the reverse. The development of clinical infection usually interrupts the normal healing process (de Haan *et al*, 1974; Bucknall, 1980; Robson *et al*, 1990) and repeated trauma, ischaemia and infection are leading causes of wound chronicity (Tarnuzzer and Schultz, 1996). Repeated infection causes elevated levels of pro-inflammatory cytokines and metalloproteinases, while bacterial enzymes degrade growth factors and extracellular matrix components. Cytotoxic bacterial toxins impair the function of many human cells intimately involved in the wound repair process. The relationship between microbial population size and delayed wound healing was first investigated in pressure ulcers, where reduction to levels below $10^6$ cfu/ml of wound exudate was required for wound healing to progress (Bendy *et al*, 1964). Another undesirable effect attributed to the presence of microorganisms in wounds is that anaerobic bacteria can give rise to malodour (Bowler *et al*, 1999).

# Isolating the culprit

Until the advent of Lister's antiseptic surgery, Galen's concept of laudable pus was generally accepted, and the development of wound infection was encouraged. Now the deleterious effects of wound infection in interrupting healing are more clearly understood and there are compelling reasons to reduce the microbial load in wounds when skin grafts are required, or where infection and/or malodour develop.

Wounds usually support polymicrobial communities, but the involvement of specific microorganisms in delayed healing has been extensively studied. *Staphylococcus aureus* is the organism most frequently isolated from wounds, and there are conflicting reports of its clinical significance. Undoubtedly it has the potential to cause infections, but it can also colonise the wound. Daltry *et al* (1981) showed that *Staphylococcus aureus* was not associated with any trend in delayed healing; in reviewing previous studies, Bowler (1998) deduced that there was no correlation between the presence of this organism and wound infection, but Madsen *et al* (1996) reported that both β-haemolytic streptococci and *Staphylococcus aureus* did contribute to delayed healing. The destructive effect of β-haemolytic streptococci to skin grafts was recognized by plastic surgeons in the 1950s (Jackson *et al*, 1951), and the need to use antimicrobial therapy to ensure their removal from chronic leg ulcers before grafting was recently reinforced (Schraibman, 1990).

*Pseudomonas aeruginosa* has been linked to enlarged venous leg ulcers (VLU) with delayed healing (Madsen *et al*, 1996) and to enlarging pressure ulcers (Daltry *et al*, 1981). This opportunist pathogen possesses a variety of virulence determinants (Lyczak *et al*, 2000), whose virulence is seen to be influenced by population density.

Another group of bacteria that have the potential to impinge on healing is the anaerobes; these possess significant virulence factors (Duerdin, 1994), and there is a correlation between the incidence of anaerobes and chronic wound infection (Bowler and Davies, 1999; Bowler *et al*, 2001).

Despite all of these observations, Trengove *et al* (1996) were unable to associate any particular type of bacterium with delayed healing, although the presence of four or more groups of bacteria did retard healing. It is possible that synergistic relationships between different species might enhance their effects on wound healing, and so there are valid arguments to reduce the levels of specific organisms in wounds, as well as total bioburden.

Whether healing in colonized wounds is influenced by bioburden is not clear. Halbert *et al* (1992) concluded that VLU colonized by bacteria were of longer duration than those that were not. It has been suggested that the microbial flora in wounds without signs of clinical infection does not influence healing (Hansson *et al*, 1995). The concept that 'bacteria in ulcers are saprophytic and will disappear when the favourable environment for their growth is lost' (Eriksson *et al*, 1984) suggests that not all microbial loads in wounds are necessarily harmful, however, it is clear that antimicrobial agents should be used selectively.

## Managing bioburden

The use of chemicals to control the growth of microorganisms in wounds has a long history, and a wide range of agents is available. Antibiotics exploit structural and functional differences between host and microbial cells, and exert relatively high selective toxicity by targeting a specific microbial process. Antiseptics and disinfectants exert a broad spectrum of activity by non-specifically affecting multiple intracellular target sites, and therefore exhibit lower selective toxicity.

Microbial inhibition is achieved by either inducing lethal events (cidal agents) or by interrupting growth without loss of viability (static agents). The removal or inactivation of static agents curtails their inhibitory effect and allows microbial growth to resume. As well as contact time, concentration and the presence of organic matter influences the effectiveness of an antimicrobial agent; these factors need consideration in wound management.

Systemic antibiotic formulations and dosage regimes are designed to maintain appropriate tissue and serum concentrations over time, but levels of topical agents (ie. in solution) will fluctuate between applications unless sustained release systems are employed. Whereas appropriately selected antibiotics are valuable in the treatment of wounds with spreading infection (Bowler *et al*, 2001), the routine use of systemic antibiotics for chronic wounds without clinical infection is not recommended (EPUAP, 1999; O'Meara *et al*, 2001; Berendt and Lipskay, 2003). Topical antimicrobials such as silver and iodine, however, may be beneficial (O'Meara *et al*, 2001). The exposure of VLU to different antiseptics has been shown to reduce mean numbers of bacteria per ulcer; but not all bacteria showed statistically significant reductions (Hansson and Faergemann, 1995).

The benefits of reducing microbial loads in wounds include the prevention of clinical infection with concomitant delays in healing, the removal of organisms destructive to skin grafts, and the removal of organisms responsible for malodour. Even the mechanical reduction in bioburden effected by wound rinsing (eg. with water or saline) is significant, but without antimicrobial agents provided in 'sustained release' formulations, population densities quickly recover. It is only by effecting a prolonged reduction in wound pathogens that the negative influence on healing can be overcome — providing an opportunity for the host immune system to regain control, and, for the healing process to resume.

With our understanding of bacterial virulence factors (Wilson *et al*, 2002) we now know that it is not always sufficient merely to kill the organism but to deal with those residual factors that can sustain pathogenicity long after the organism is dead — this is a therapeutic paradox (Miragliotta, 1991). Specifically, bacterial endotoxins, which are released upon disruption of the bacterial cell can be harmful for the healing process (Metzger *et al*, 2002; Kawaguchi *et al*, 1995) and can lead to increased morbidity (Miragliotta, 1991; Dudley, 1990). Endotoxins are typically released from Gram-negative bacteria. To date, only one wound dressing has been associated with endotoxin removal. Actisorb Silver 220 has been evaluated in an *in vitro* study using *Escherichia coli* (Müller *et al*, 2003). Using *Escherichia coli* endotoxin 055;B5, Müller *et al* showed the dressing to adsorb significant amounts of endotoxin in a time-dependent basis. In a clinical context, this toxin-binding effect is likely to be beneficial as bacterial toxin (admittedly *Pseudomonas aeruginosa* exotoxin A) has been related to ulcer deterioration (Danielsen *et al*, 1998).

AS220 is indicated for the treatment of wet or dry infected and malodorous wounds (*Chapter 10* [Hampton, 2001]; Johnson & Johnson Medical Ltd, 2001a); it has no significant absorptive capacity, and is not designed to take up wound exudate. An absorbent secondary dressing is therefore required on wet wounds. AS220 has been shown to be effective against both Gram-positive and Gram-negative organisms *in vitro* (Furr *et al*, 1994). Silver (in metallic and salt forms) is known to have broad-spectrum activity against a wide range of microorganisms (*Chapter 7* [White, 2001]).

With the current interest in silver in the control of wound colonization and infection, and concerns regarding the use of topical antibiotics, it is appropriate to review the clinical data on Actisorb Silver 220.

## Comparative studies

The first published comparative study involving Actisorb was that by Mulligan *et al* (1986). This community-based study was conducted on the original, non-silver Actisorb. A total of 101 subjects were randomised by a computer generated system to either Actisorb or to 'control', ie. any other dressing that the investigator felt appropriate. Treatment was for six weeks, or until healing. Parameters measured included ulcer size and condition (granulation tissue, exudate level, oedema, odour, pain), and the number of dressings used. Data were subjected to statistical analysis by either Mann Whitney or Chi-squared tests.

Information was obtained on sixty-five subjects randomized to Actisorb and thirty-two randomized to 'control' dressings. There were no statistically significant differences in baseline demographic data such as patient age, gender, and ulcer size, although the Actisorb group included ulcers of longer mean duration (117 *vs* 52 months) and larger mean area (30.3cm$^2$ *vs* 19.7cm$^2$).

The Actisorb group used marginally fewer primary dressings than the control group and achieved a greater mean reduction in ulcer area (1.2cm$^2$ per week *vs* 0.2cm$^2$) but these were not statistically significant. During the six-week treatment period the Actisorb group showed a statistically significant mean percentage reduction in ulcer size of 28.7% (SEM 3.95) compared to the control group 11.7% (SEM 6.77). Actisorb was statistically superior for increased epithelialization, and reduced exudate, odour and oedema levels (p=0.005). There were no differences detected in pain levels.

The investigators felt they had contravened the randomization to some degree in order to evaluate the new dressing on the 'worst' (ie. greater prognostic healing factors) ulcers — this would explain the greater surface area and duration of wounds in this group. Nevertheless, the Actisorb group achieved statistically significantly greater percentage area reduction in the treatment period. This apparent bias would tend to reduce or even eliminate the likelihood of a false positive. While Actisorb is not an exudate-absorbent dressing, the significant reduction in exudate levels can be attributed to the capacity of the charcoal cloth component to adsorb bacteria, so reducing infection and indirectly, exudate levels.

In the UK, Millward (1991) compared Actisorb Plus with two control dressings (a chlorhexidine paraffin gauze and a charcoal dressing) on sixty community-based patients with leg ulcers. All wounds were swabbed at weekly intervals for two weeks before the study start, and for four weeks with the test dressings in use. Wounds were assessed subjectively at each dressing change according to a standard scale. The overall assessments of dressing performance showed Actisorb Plus to be 'very effective' in wound cleansing, malodour control and exudate reduction (by virtue of the antibacterial effects). It also performed well clinically, with all treated wounds showing healing improvement. Importantly for community use and cost-effectiveness, the overall wear time was extended compared to the control dressings and to previous treatments.

In Germany, two studies have been conducted using silver-impregnated Actisorb. In the first (Wunderlich and Orfanos, 1991), forty patients with chronic VLU were randomized to either conventional (zinc paste bandages) or test (Actisorb Plus) therapy. During the six-week treatment period, wound parameters were measured (ulcer size, odour, necrotic tissue, epithelialization, erythema, oedema).

Nineteen patients completed the treatment period in each group. For the important healing parameters of decrease in ulcer size and increase in epithelialization, Actisorb Plus was statistically superior to the control (p<0.05). In the group treated with Actisorb Plus, six ulcers (32%) healed compared with two (10%) in the control group. For all other parameters, there were no significant differences detected. Important 'in use' characteristics of the dressing that became evident in this study were low adherence to the wound, and from the patient perspective its softness and conformability.

In the second, prospective non-comparative study, Tebbe and Orfanos (1996) treated 156 patients with leg ulcers and sixty-eight with pressure ulcers with Actisorb Plus for four weeks. This study combined a clinical evaluation of the dressing in terms of performance in reducing exudate, promoting granulation and re-epithelialization with an *in vitro* antibacterial assay. The dressing was retrospectively compared to the previous, 'phase-related' (symptomatic) treatment in terms of wear time, dressing change time, and healing parameters.

According to Tebbe and Orfanos, the proportion of methicillin-resistant *Staphylococcus aureus* (MRSA) in all staphylococcal isolates in Germany is 3–5% and increasing. MRSA is currently sensitive to systemic vancomycin and teicoplanin, or to topical mupirocin (although this last is ineffective against *Pseudomonas aeruginosa*). Tebbe and Orfanos maintained that modern wound treatments can be useful in treating wound infections and that an ideal antibacterial dressing will be broad spectrum, and effective against MRSA.

All patients enrolled into the study had demographic details recorded as well as wound specific information: area, condition, duration, previous treatments, wear times and others. A total of 224 patients were enrolled of which over 25% had either diabetes and/or peripheral circulatory disorders. Eight patients (3.5%) withdrew during the study and 218 (96.5%) completed. Two withdrawals (0.9%) were for suspected adverse events — one case of peri-wound erythema and one of wound pain. All others were unrelated to the dressing. The average age of patients was 65.2 years and most were male (161, 72%). The average size and duration of wounds was 24.2cm$^2$/20 months for VLU and 28.1cm$^2$/6.7 months for pressure ulcers. Of these wounds, 1.9% of VLU and 1.5% of pressure ulcers showed signs of granulation at the start of treatment. Epithelialization was evident in 1.3% of all leg ulcers and in no pressure ulcers at the start of treatment.

The results showed that the average number of dressing changes was reduced in both groups; in leg ulcers this reduced from 6.2 at the start to 3.6 times per week, and in pressure ulcers from 8.9 to 4.4. Dressing change time was also reduced, from an average of 8.8 and 9.6 minutes for leg ulcers and pressure ulcers respectively, to 7.7 and 6.4 minutes.

The wound size in both groups was significantly reduced by treatment ($p<0.01$) to a mean of 13.4 cm$^2$ for leg ulcers and 13.0 cm$^2$ for pressure ulcers. Granulation increased to 81.2% of leg ulcers and 68.6% of pressure ulcers. Epithelialization increased to 81% of leg ulcers and to 69.2% of pressure ulcers.

The authors suggested that Actisorb Plus (AS220) can be used as a multi-phase therapy, ie. used throughout the duration of the wound. In addition to the positive healing and safety outcomes, a cost-benefit advantage was claimed on the basis of increased wear time, decreased dressing change time, and superior clinical performance.

These results are consistent with the findings of Cassino *et al* (2001), who compared systemic antibiotic therapy with topical antisepsis (AS220) in chronic wounds with localised infection. A total of 150 patients with a range of infected chronic wounds (according to the criteria of Cutting and Harding [1994]) were randomized to either treatment (*Table 9.1*). Preliminary results showed both treatments to be very effective, however, the topical approach proved to be more cost-effective, and, somewhat surprisingly, to lead to fewer recurrences in the short term.

**Table 9.1: Cost analysis of treatment of chronic wounds treated with Actisorb Plus and antibiotics**

|  | Actisorb group (n=75) | Antibiotics group (n=75) |
|---|---|---|
| Global costs ($) | 1542.85 | 9898.57 |
| Average daily cost ($) | 110.20 | 932.55 |
| Average daily coss per patient ($) | 1.45 | 12.43 |
| Effectiveness (%) | 94.6 | 97.3 |
| Average treatment period (days) | 14 | 10.4 |
| Recurrences within thirty days (%) | 1.3 | 12.0 |

Source: Cassino *et al*, 2001

In France, Bornier and Jeanin (1989) conducted a non-comparative study on Actisorb Plus in a group of patients with chronic and acute wounds. The objective was to study the effect of the dressing on wound infection, and tolerance to the dressing. The Actisorb Plus was changed every two days and covered, as required, with absorbent secondary dressings. Twenty subjects were recruited, with an average age of seventy-nine years (range 62–93); seventeen female, three male. Four had acute wounds and sixteen chronic wounds, including nine venous and arterial leg ulcers and seven pressure ulcers. Previous, ineffective treatments included tulle gras and iodinated dressings. In each case, the use of Actisorb Plus resulted in the rapid resolution of the infection.

## Surveillance studies

As part of the requirements of German drug law, a number of open, multicentre, observational 'in use' studies (Anwendungsbeobach-tung) have been conducted by family physicians (GPs). These are similar in design and objective to post-marketing surveillance studies (PMS) or Safety Assessment of Marketed Medicines (SAMM) in the UK. (It is important to recognize that in Germany, unlike in the UK, wound care is a physician-led discipline.)

A standard case report form was used to obtain baseline information on patient demographics, wound type, duration, dimensions, characteristics, previous treatments and outcomes, and intercurrent illnesses.

Five studies were conducted between 1996 and 2000 (Johnson & Johnson Ltd, 2001b), recruiting a total of 12,444 consenting patients with a range of non-healing chronic (defined as lack of response to previous treatment) and acute wounds (*Table 9.2*). Patients were treated for six or twelve weeks, or until healed. A brief summary of results is presented here; a detailed publication of these data is available (Actisorb 2003).

### Table 9.2: Wound types in PMS six- and twelve-week studies

| Wound type | Number of patients | % |
|---|---|---|
| Pressure ulcer | 2435 | 19.6 |
| Venous leg ulcer | 7798 | 62.7 |
| Diabetic foot ulcer | 1493 | 12.0 |
| Acute wounds* | 718 | 5.8 |

* Traumatic 294 (41%); post-operative 180 (25%); other 244 (34%)

Data were pooled for analysis purposes; this was justified on the basis of a single protocol used throughout. All interval scaled parameters were analysed descriptively for the relevant subgroups and presented with the following metrics:

- number of data (n)
- arithmetic mean and standard deviation (SD)
- median, minimum and maximum
- ninety-five per cent confidence intervals.

Nominally and ordinally scaled parameters were presented with their absolute and relative frequencies in percentages.

The demographic profile of the patient population shows approximately 60% were female, with a mean age of sixty-seven years. Almost 32% were diabetic. The median wound duration on enrolment was three months with an average wound radius of 2.2 cm (approximately 15 cm$^2$ area) in pressure ulcers, 2.6 cm in VLU (approximately 22 cm$^2$), and 2.0 cm in diabetic foot ulcers (approximately 12.6 cm$^2$). While most VLU were superficial, all other types of wounds were predominantly deep or deep with sinus.

Previous treatments for the wound included hydrocolloids (15.6%) and plain/antimicrobial gauzes (84.1%) and the main reason for switching therapy was 'lack of efficacy' in 83% of patients.

In the course of the studies, side-effects (adverse events) were reported in 361 patients (2.9%). The most frequent were pain (103, 0.83%), burning sensation (71, 0.57%), general intolerance (30, 0.24%) and erythema (15, 0.12%). In ten subjects, 'infection' was documented as an adverse event. The subject preference on tolerability was 'much better' than previous in 40% and 'better' in 31%. Treatment was prematurely terminated in 666 subjects (5.4%), mainly for lack of improvement (107, 0.86%) and intolerance (52, 0.42%). With the very large sample numbers involved, these adverse event data should be viewed favourably.

The overall healing rate after six weeks was 35.5% and after twelve weeks, 49.3% (*Table 9.3*). The healing rate for acute wounds was greater at each time point than for chronic wounds, as may be expected.

| Table 9.3: Treatment outcome: change from baseline (six-week studies only*) | | | | | |
|---|---|---|---|---|---|
| **Wound type** | **Number of wounds** | **Healed *n* (%)** | **Improved *n* (%)** | **Worse *n* (%)** | **NA *n* (%)** |
| Pressure ulcer | 2081 | 496 (23.8) | 796 (38.3) | 12 (0.6) | 290 (13.9) |
| Venous leg ulcer | 6732 | 1422 (21.1) | 2349 (34.9) | 25 (0.4) | 1280 (19.0) |
| Diabetic foot ulcer | 855 | 322 (24.8) | 445 (34.2) | 2 (0.2) | 276 (21.2) |
| Traumatic/ acute | 389 | 324 (56.4) | 132 (23.0) | 1 (0.2) | 41 (7.1) |
| Total | 10 057 | 2564 (25.5) | 3722 (37.0) | 40 (0.4) | 1887 (18.8) |

* This time period was selected as being more appropriate for the management of infected wounds than twelve weeks; NA = not applicable

## Discussion

This review of published clinical trial data on Actisorb dressings, with and without silver, provides the current evidence basis for clinical judgment. The original, non-silver, Actisorb has been shown to be effective in reducing wound malodour and in removing bacteria from the wound. Even without an antimicrobial ingredient, the dressing reduces wound bioburden and can, consequently, be said to be of value in infection control (Bowler *et al*, 1999). The addition of silver has been demonstrated to be an effective antibacterial measure *in vitro* (Furr *et al*, 1994). Clinical efficacy and safety has been demonstrated in three small studies in the UK and France, a large on-going study in Italy, and in two large trials in Germany. The findings from these studies are supported by the very large, non-comparative, PMS study also conducted in Germany. The positive healing and reduction of infection data obtained in these studies can be attributed largely to the effects of the dressing as the majority of patients received no other antibacterial treatment (*Table 9.4*).

| Table 9.4: Concomitant treatment of infections | | | | |
|---|---|---|---|---|
| **Wound type** | **None** | **Topical** | **Systemic** | **Other** |
| Pressure ulcer | 78.6% | 3.0% | 7.4% | 11.0% |
| Leg ulcer | 79.8% | 3.0% | 6.0% | 11.2% |
| Diabetic foot | 70.3% | 4.1% | 15.8% | 9.9% |
| Acute | 77.0% | 3.3% | 9.5% | 10.3% |

The preliminary findings of the study conducted by Cassino's group in Italy raise fundamental questions about the principles and practice of infected wound management. Their results suggest that where chronic wounds such as leg ulcers are locally infected, ie. there is no spreading infection, then systemic antibiotics are not necessarily required. This is consistent with other recent reports (EPUAP, 1999; Bowler *et al*, 2001). Furthermore, the objections to topical antibacterial therapy defined by Selwyn (1981) do not apply to AS220. It has no record of local tissue damage, no associated systemic toxicity, no reports of contact sensitivity or other allergic reactions, and no evidence of resistance or super-infection (invasion by bacteria resistant to the therapy in use complicating the course of antimicrobial therapy of an existing infectious process).

These phenomena are all associated with topical antibiotics and some other antiseptic agents (White *et al*, 2001). It is important, therefore, to differentiate topical antibiotics from topical antiseptics, and further to separate those topical antiseptics — particularly in solution formulations — that can provoke unwanted local and systemic responses (Rodeheaver, 1990a,b; Moore, 1992; Lawrence, 1998; Kaye, 2000).

The principles of clinical governance incorporate the need for evidence-based practice. This is supported by clinical and cost-effectiveness, and evidence of safety, ie. clinical risk management. While the evidence presented in this review of clinical trials does not meet the 'gold standard' requirements in every case, five studies are randomised and controlled and two are non-comparative. The wealth of data from these studies, particularly the latter two, is testimony to the safety and efficacy of Actisorb Silver 220, albeit from some non-comparative research. The overriding conclusion is that the dressing is, on the basis of substantial evidence acquired over fifteen years of sales and research, a safe and effective multi-phase product for the treatment of infected and malodorous wounds.

# Key points

❖ Silver, as metal or colloidal form, is known to be an effective antimicrobial *in vitro* and *in vivo*.

❖ Charcoal fabric has been used for many years to control malodour.

❖ The charcoal cloth in original Actisorb and Actisorb Silver 220 adsorbs bacteria, effectively removing them from the wound environment. Evidence from a comparative clinical trial shows Actisorb Silver 220 to be effective in the treatment of chronic wounds.

❖ Clinical studies involving Actisorb Silver 220 demonstrate healing, infection and odour control, and good 'in use' characteristics.

❖ Preliminary evidence is accumulating on the comparative cost-effectiveness of Actisorb Silver 220 over systemic antibiotics in infected chronic wounds.

❖ Substantial evidence from non-comparative studies involving many thousands of patients confirms the value of Actisorb Silver 220 as a safe and effective dressing in a variety of acute and chronic wounds.

# References

Actisorb Product Monograph Ethicon GmbH Johnson & Johnson Wound Management 2003

Bendy RH, Nuccio PA, Wolfe E *et al* (1964) Relationship of quantitative bacterial counts to healing of decubiti. *Antimicrob Agents Chemother* **4**: 147–55

Berendt T, Lipskay BA (2003) Should antibiotics be used in the treatment of the diabetic foot? *The Diabetic Foot* **6**(1): 18–28

Bornier C, Jeannin C (1989) Clinical trials with ACTISORB (Etude clinique Actisorb. Realisee sur 20 cas plaies complexes). *Soins Chir* **99**: 39–41

Bornside GH, Bornside BB (1979) Comparison between moist swab and tissue biopsy methods for bacteria in experimental incision wounds. *J Trauma* **19**: 103–5

Bowler PG (1998) The anaerobic and aerobic microbiology of wounds: a review. *Wounds* **10**: 170–8

Bowler PG, Davies BJ, Jones SA (1999) Microbial involvement in wound malodour. *J Wound Care* **8**: 216–8

Bowler PG, Davies BJ (1999) The microbiology of acute and chronic wounds. *Wounds* **11**: 72–9

Bowler PG, Duerden BI, Armstrong DG (2001) Wound microbiology and associated approaches to wound management. *Clin Microbiol Rev* **14**(2): 244–69

Breidenbach WC, Trager S (1995) Quantitative culture technique and infection in complex wounds of the extremities closed with free flaps. *Plast Reconstr Surg* **95**: 860–5

Bucknall TE (1980) The effect of local infection upon wound healing: an experimental study. *Br J Surg* **67**: 851–5

Cassino R, Ricci E, Carusone A (2001) *Management of infected wounds: a review of antibiotic and antiseptic treatments*. Poster presentation European Wound Management Association, Dublin, 17–19 May

Cooper R, Lawrence JC (1996) Microorganisms and wounds. *J Wound Care* **5**(5): 233–6

Cutting KF, Harding KG (1994) Criteria for identifying wound infection. *J Wound Care* **3**(4): 198–201

Cutting KF (2001) A dedicated follower of fashion? Topical medications and wounds. *Br J Nurs* **10**(15 Silver Supplement): S9–S16

Daltry DC, Rhodes B, Chattwood JG (1981) Investigation into the microbial flora of healing and non-healing decubitus ulcers. *J Clin Pathol* **34**: 701–5

Danielsen L, Balslev E, Doring G *et al* (1998) Ulcer bed infection. *APMIS* **106**: 721–6

de Haan BB, Ellis H, Wilks M (1974) The role of infection on wound healing. *Surg Gynecol Obstetr* **138**: 693–700

Dudley MN (1990) Overview of Gram-negative sepsis. *Am J Hosp Pharm* **47**(suppl 3): S3–S6

Duerdin BI (1994) Virulence factors in anaerobes. *Clin Infect Dis* **18**(Suppl): S253–S259

Elek SD (1956) Experimental staphylococcal infections in the skin of man. *Ann NY Acad Sci* **65**: 85–90

Emmerson M (1998) A microbiologist's view of factors contributing to infection. *New Horizons* **6**(2 Suppl): S3–S10

Eriksson G, Eklund A-E, Kallings LO (1984) The clinical significance of bacterial growth in venous leg ulcers. *Scand J Infect Dis* **16**: 175–80

European Pressure Ulcer Advisory Panel (1999) Guidelines on the treatment of pressure ulcers. *EPUAP Rev* **1**: 31–3

Furr JR, Russell AD, Turner TD, Andrews A (1994) Antibacterial activity of Actisorb Plus, Actisorb and silver nitrate. *J Hosp Infect* **27**: 201–8

Halbert AR, Stacey MC, Rohr JB *et al* (1992) The effect of bacterial colonization on venous ulcer healing. *Aust J Dermatol* **33**: 75080

Hampton S (2001) Actisorb Silver 220: a unique antibacterial dressing. *Br J Nurs* **10**(15 Silver Supplement): 17–19

Hansson CJ, Faergemann J (1995) The effect of antiseptic solutions on micro-organisms in venous leg ulcers. *Acta Dermato-Venereol* (Stockh) **75**: 31–3

Hansson CJ, Holborn A, Moller A, Swanbeck G (1995) The microbial flora in venous leg ulcers without signs of clinical infection. *Acta Dermato-Venereol* (Stockh) **75**: 452–6

Hepburn HH (1919) Delayed primary suture of wounds. *Br Med J* **I**: 181–3

Johnson & Johnson Medical Ltd (2001a) Actisorb Silver 220. Product Literature document JJM 1066. J & J, Ascot

Johnson & Johnson Medical Ltd (2001b) Post Marketing Surveillance Studies Actisorb 1996–2000; Therapy of chronic wounds. (Data on file)

Jackson DM, Lowbury EJL, Topley E (1951) Chemotherapy of Streptococcus infection in burns. *Lancet* **2**: 705–11

Kawaguchi H, Hizuta A, Tanaka N, Orita K (1995) Role of endotoxin in wound healing impairment. *Res Commun Mol Pathol Pharmacol* **89**: 317–27

Kaye ET (2000) Topical antibacterial agents. *Infect Dis Clin N Am* **14**(2): 321–39

Kingsley A (2001) A proactive approach to wound infection. *Nurs Standard* **15**(30): 50–8

Krizek TJ, Robson MC, Kho E (1967) Bacterial growth and skin graft survival. *Surg Forum* **18**: 518–9

Lawrence JC (1998) The use of iodine as an antiseptic agent. *J Wound Care* **7**(8): 421–5

Leaper (1998) Defining infection (Editorial). *J Wound Care* **7**(8): 373

Lookingbill DP, Miller SH, Knowles RC (1978) Bacteriology of chronic leg ulcers. *Arch Dermatol* **114**: 1765–8

Lyczak JB, Cannon CL, Pier GB (2000) *Pseudomonas aeruginosa* infection: lessons from a versatile opportunist. *Microbes Infect* **2**(9): 1051–60

Madsen SM, Westh H, Danielsen L, Rosdahl VT (1996) Bacterial colonization and healing of venous leg ulcers. *APMIS* **104**: 895–9

Metzger Z, Nitzan D, Pitaru S, Brosh T, Teicher S (2002) The effect of bacterial endotoxin on the early tensile strength of healing surgical wounds. *J Endodon* **28**: 30–3

Millward P (1991) Comparing treatments for leg ulcers. *Nurs Times* **87**(13): 70–2

Miragliotta G (1991) Endotoxin release after antibiotic treatment and its potential pathogenic role in coagulative disorders of patients with Gram-negative sepsis. *J Chemoter* **3** (suppl 1): 69–72

Moore D (1992) Hypochlorites: a review of the evidence. *J Wound Care* **1**(4): 44–53

Mulligan CM, Bragg AJ, O'Toole OB (1986) A controlled comparative trial of Actisorb activated charcoal cloth dressing in the community. *Br J Clin Pract* **40**: 145–8

O'Meara SM, Cullum NA, Majid M, Sheldon TA (2001) Systematic review of antimicrobial agents used for chronic wounds. *Br J Surg* **88**: 4–21

Raahave D, Friis-Moller A, Bjerre-Jespen K, Rasmussen LB (1986) The infective dose of aerobic and anaerobic bacteria in post-operative wound sepsis. *Arch Surg* **121**: 924–9

Raju DR, Jindrak K, Weiner M, Endquist IF (1977) A study of the critical bacterial innoculum to cause a stimulus to wound healing. *Surg Gynecol Obstetr* **144**: 347–50

Robson M, Heggers JP (1969) Bacterial quantification of open wounds. *Mil Med* **134**: 19–24

Robson M, Heggers JP (1970) Delayed wound closure based on bacterial counts. *J Surg Oncol* **2**(4): 379–83

Robson M, Steinberg BD, Heggers JP (1990) Wound healing alterations caused by infection. *Clin Plast Surg* **17**: 485–92

Rodeheaver G (1990a) Influence of antiseptics on wound healing. In: Alexander JW, Hutchinson JJ, eds. *International Forum on Wound Microbiology*. Excerpta Medica, Princeton USA

Rodeheaver G (1990b) Controversies in topical wound management: wound cleansing and wound disinfection. In: Krasner D, ed. *Chronic Wound Care*. Pennsylvania Health Management Publications, USA

Schraibman IG (1990) The significance of β-haemolytic streptococci in chronic leg ulcers. *Ann Royal Coll Surg Eng* **72**: 123–4

Selwyn S (1981) The topical treatment of skin infections. In: Maibach H, Aly R, eds. *Skin Microbiology: Relevance to Clinical Infection*. Springer Verlag, New York

Tarnuzzer RW, Schultz GS (1996) Biochemical analysis of acute and chronic wound environments. *Wound Rep Regen* **4**: 411–20

Tebbe B, Orfanos CE (1996) Therapy of leg ulcers and decubitus ulcers with a xero-dressing: Modern wound dressing with antibacterial activity. *H+G Band* **71**(9): 697–702

Tenorio A, Jindrak, Weiner M (1976) Accelerated healing in infected wounds. *Surg Gynecol Obstet* **142**: 537–43

Teplitz C, Davis D, Mason AD, Moncrief JA (1964) *Pseudomonas aeruginosa* burn wound sepsis. *J Surg Res* **4**: 200–16

Trengove NJ, Stacey MC, McGechie DF, Mata S (1996) Qualitative bacteriology and leg ulcer healing. *J Wound Care* **5**: 277–80

White RJ, Cooper R, Kingsley A (2001) Wound colonization and infection: the role of topical antimicrobials. *Br J Nurs* **10**(9): 563–77

White RJ (2001) An historical overview of the use of silver in wound management. *Br J Nurs* **10**(15 Silver Supplement): 3–8

Wilson JW, Schurr MJ, LeBlanc CL, Ramamurthy R, Buchanan KL, Nickerson CA (2002) Mechanisms of bacterial pathogenicity. *Postgrad Med J* **78**: 216–24

Wunderlich U, Orfanos CE (1991) Treatment of venous leg ulcers with silver-impregnated zero-dressings. *Hautartz* **42**: 446–50

# 10

# Actisorb Silver 220: a unique antibacterial dressing

*Sylvie Hampton*

The antibacterial function of the unique dressing Actisorb Silver 220 (manufactured by Johnson & Johnson Medical) is growing in importance as methicillin-resistant bacteria increase in prevalence and as the efficacy of antibiotics becomes more limited. Consequently, practitioners need to look elsewhere for solutions to managing wound colonization and in prevention of clinical infections. Actisorb Silver 220 assists with cleansing the wound, reduces malodour, and has the ability to reduce bacterial colonization in wet and dry wounds: all are vital functions for wound healing, improvement of patients' quality of life, and in reducing healthcare costs.

Provision of the optimum wound healing environment is one of the most crucial determinants of wound closure rate and is founded on the practitioner's ability to select the most appropriate dressing. The required skill is in the provision of an individualized and ideal healing environment for each patient. Selection of an appropriate dressing requires knowledge of both the art (clinical experience) and the science (evidence-based knowledge) of wound care, with the ultimate wound care decisions being based on holistic assessment of the patient.

For a patient with a wound, the principal problem may not be the wound itself, but rather associated quality of life-related issues such as pain, exudate leakage and malodour. A knowledgeable and thorough assessment should disclose these issues, whereupon they may be addressed specifically in management. This will help the patient to adjust better psychologically to the wound.

## Wound microbiology

One of the main functions of healthy skin is to protect the underlying structures from being invaded by potential pathogens (Bowler *et al*, 2001). Once the dermis is breached, there is opportunity for the entry of bacteria into the warm, moist environment — ideal for bacterial growth and colonization. The healthy skin is host to many microorganisms, many of which are harmless commensals although some may be potential pathogens.

All chronic wounds are very likely to be colonized as the opportunistic bacteria succeed in entering the wound environment and establishing a state of colonization or infection (Bowler *et al*, 2001). There is, however, some debate on the importance of colonizing bacteria and whether they are likely to influence (ie. delay) wound healing (Eriksson *et al*, 1984; Annoni *et al*, 1989). Nevertheless,

Harding (1996) states that:

*Work cited as long ago as 1970 suggests that optimal wound healing cannot be achieved unless bacteria are eliminated from wounds.*

Although, in reality, this is most unlikely to be achieved.

Danielson *et al* (1997) suggest that extracellular toxins produced by bacteria might interfere with the healing process, with the responsible bacterial enzymes and matrix metalloproteinases degrading fibrin and wound growth factors.

Bendy *et al* (1964) reported that healing in pressure ulcers progressed only when the bacterial load was less than $10^6$ colony-forming units (CFU)/ml of wound fluid. This leads to the general conclusion that wounds will heal faster when bacterial contamination is reduced and clinical infection will be eliminated if bacterial load is maintained at less than $10^6$ CFU/ml of wound fluid. In practice, the initiation of appropriate treatment at an early stage is intended to interrupt the infection continuum (Kingsley, 2001) and so avoid the expensive sequelae of infection, morbidity and increased management costs (Green and Wenzel, 1977; Plowman, 2000).

The presence of microorganisms in wounds can provoke an increase in exudate levels and malodour. Wound care decisions may be directed towards managing these symptoms rather than treating and reducing the colonization or infection that is causing the problem. Wounds that are colonized by bacteria are not necessarily clinically infected and administration of systemic antibiotics for uninfected wounds is both pointless and dangerous as it increases the potential sensitization and selection of resistant strains (Huovinen *et al*, 1994; Zaki *et al*, 1994).

However, the presence of wound microorganisms can develop into clinical infection if the host immunological response is in any way compromised, or if the bacterial bioburden (load) becomes greater than $10^5$–$10^6$ per gram of tissue or millilitre of exudate (Cutting, 1998; Robson, 1999; Miller, 2001). It is possible for this bioburden to be reduced and clinical infection avoided by the judicious use of topical antibacterial agents such as silver and iodine (White *et al*, 2001).

## Silver as a topical antimicrobial

The antibacterial properties of silver have been known and applied for centuries (Russell and Hugo, 1994) and have been used for eye infections, internal infections and burns. Silver produces structural changes within the bacterial cells and interacts with nucleic acids while also acting as a heavy metal by impairing the bacterial electron system and some bacterial DNA functions (Russell and Hugo, 1994).

There are numerous important functional proteins, such as enzymes, within the bacterial cell, and many of these enzymes are responsible for the transport of vital nutrients in and out of the bacterial cell. Silver penetrates the organism by binding strongly to these enzymes and inhibiting their transporting function.

Silver will also disrupt the bacterial cell membrane, leading to cell death. Silver is a broad-spectrum bactericidal and is particularly useful in Gram-negative organisms such as *Pseudomonas aeruginosa* (Parker, 1993).

Given that two of the particular difficulties facing wound patients are exudate and malodour, any dressing that can reduce the bacterial bioburden, and hence the odour, will be valuable. As exudate is also closely related to wound bacteria, reduction in colonization and infection will also reduce exudate (White, 2001). The Actisorb Silver 220 dressing has been produced to address these problems.

## Actisorb Silver 220

Actisorb Silver 220 (formerly known as Actisorb Plus) is a unique wound dressing that contains an activated charcoal cloth combined with silver and offers a triple action:

- it is antibacterial with a broad spectrum of activity against bacteria and fungi (Russell and Hugo, 1994)
- reduces malodour by eliminating those bacteria that give rise to the problem, and by adsorption of odour molecules onto the activated charcoal layer
- adsorption of bacterial endotoxins (Müller *et al*, 2003).

The carbon element of Actisorb Silver 220 is able to adsorb small gas and liquid molecules (Coombs, 1981) and this filters the malodour, thus acting as a deodorizer. The cloth within Actisorb Silver 220 has an adsorbent capacity that is twenty times greater than that of traditional materials (Williams, 1994). At the same time, the charcoal adsorbs bacteria and their spores, which attach themselves to the charcoal filaments (Coombs, 1981), presenting an ideal situation for the antibacterial silver component to interact. Bacterial toxins are part of the virulence factors that contribute to pathogenicity. Endotoxins are bacterial cell wall components that are released on cell lysis. They have been linked to impaired wound healing (Danielson *et al*, 1997). Müller *et al* (2003) have demonstrated endotoxin binding by Actisorb Silver 220 in an *in vitro* study.

Actisorb Silver 220 is indicated for the management of exuding infected wounds such as leg ulcers (it is effective under compression bandaging), pressure ulcers, and fungating wounds.

Mulligan and O'Toole (1986) undertook a large study in leg ulceration and found that Actisorb Silver 220 absorbs wound exudate and odour as well as bacteria. Milward (1991) reviewed the clinical use of three dressings: paraffin gauze; a carbon dressing; and Actisorb Silver 220. It was found that Actisorb Silver 220 was the most effective dressing for wound cleansing, malodour control, exudate control and rate of healing. Milward also found that dressing change rate was greatly reduced.

This, combined with the findings of Wunderlich and Orfanos (1991), who found faster healing in venous leg ulcers, has an impact on cost, making Actisorb Silver 220 a cost-effective option for reducing bacterial colonization and malodour. The dressing has been evaluated in leg ulcers and pressure ulcers in a large study (over 200 patients) by Tebbe and Orfanos (1996). They found the dressing to be effective in reducing wound size and bacterial contamination.

The activated charcoal cloth of Actisorb Silver 220 is held within a non-adherent spun-bonded nylon sleeve which should be placed directly against the wound (Williams, 1994). The author has often found that Actisorb is used as a secondary dressing and placed over the primary dressing (often foam) to absorb odours. This is a pointless and wasteful exercise as the foam will only absorb fluid, and Actisorb Silver 220 has far greater capabilities with a strong rationale for use as the primary dressing.

In leg ulceration, Actisorb Silver 220 can be used under compression and can be left in place for seven days. However, this may be debated in the light of a heavy bacterial colonization as the dressing would be used as treatment and the wound condition may dictate more frequent dressing changes. However, if left in place for seven days, a secondary dressing may be used and changed whenever strikethrough occurs (Williams, 1994).

Actisorb Silver 220 is also an extremely attractive option for malodorous fungating wounds as the malodour and bacterial contamination can be controlled without using bulky dressings. Once again, secondary dressings may be used as a support if the wound is producing copious exudate.

## Conclusion

Actisorb Silver 220 is a dressing that provides effective treatment for wound colonization and infection as well as managing malodour and exudate. In the current climate of cost control in health care and of ever-increasing resistance to antibiotics, Actisorb Silver 220 has a developing and important role to play in wound management.

## Key points

* ❖ Actisorb Silver 220 is a unique dressing which has a powerful role in reducing wound bacterial colonization.
* ❖ Patient quality of life can be effected by pain, high exudate and malodour. Actisorb Silver 220 adsorbs exudate and malodour and removes the cause of these problems through bactericidal action.

❖ Silver produces structural changes within bacterial cells and interacts with nucleic acids while also acting as a heavy metal, impairing the bacterial electron transport system and some of the DNA functions, leading to bacterial cell death.

❖ The carbon component of Actisorb Silver 220 is able to adsorb small gas and liquid odour molecules. This reduces the malodour, thus acting as a deodorizer.

❖ The ability to cleanse wounds, absorb fluid and kill bacteria establishes Actisorb Silver 220 as an ideal dressing in wound care.

# References

Annoni F, Rosina D, Chiurazzi, Ceva M (1989) The effects of a hydrocolloid dressing on bacterial growth and the healing process of leg ulcers. *Int Angiol* **8**: 224–8

Bendy RH, Nuccio P, Wolfe E (1964) Relationship of quantitative wound bacterial counts to healing of decubiti: effect of topical gentamicin. *Antimicrob Agents Chemother* **4**: 147–55

Bowler PG, Duerden BI, Armstrong DG (2001) Wound microbiology and associated approaches to wound management. *Clin Microbiol Rev* **14**(2): 244–69

Coombs TJ (1981) More than a wound dressing. *Health Soc Serv J* **91**(4768): 1268–9

Cutting KF (1998) *Wounds and Infection*. Wound Care Society, London: 2

Danielson L, Cherry GW, Harding K, Rollman O (1997) Cadexomer iodine in ulcers colonized by *Pseudomonas aeruginosa*. *J Wound Care* **6**(4): 169–72

Green J, Wenzel R (1977) Postoperative wound infection: a controlled study of the increased duration of hospital stay and direct costs of hospitalization. *Ann Surg* **185**(3): 264–8

Eriksson F, Eklund A, Kallings LO (1984) The clinical significance of bacterial growth in venous leg ulcers. *Scand J Infect Dis* **16**: 175–80

Harding K (1996) The use of antiseptics in wound care. *J Wound Care* **5**(1): 44–7

Kingsley A (2001) A proactive approach to wound infection. *Nurs Standard* **15**(30): 50–8

Miller M (2001) Wound infection unravelled. *J Community Nurs* **15**(3): 31–6

Milward P (1991) Comparing treatments for leg ulcers. *Nurs Times* **87**(13): 70–2

Müller G, Winkler Y, Kramer A (2003) Antibacterial activity and endotoxin-binding capacity of Actisorb Silver 220. *J Hosp Infect* **53**(3): 211–14

Mulligan CM, O'Toole OB (1986) A controlled comparative trial of Actisorb activated charcoal cloth dressing in the community. *Br J Clin Pract* **9**(1): 145–8

Parker JA (1993) *Burns*. Education leaflet, Wound Care Society, Hungtindon: 14

Plowman R (2000) *The Socio-economics Burden of Hospital-acquired Infection: Executive Summary*. Public Health Laboratory Service, London

Robson MC (1999) Lessons gleaned from the sport of wound watching. *Wound Repair Regen* **7**(1): 2–6

Russell AD, Hugo WB (1994) Antimicrobial activity and action of silver. *Prog Med Chem* **31**: 351–70

Tebbe B, Orfanos CE (1996) Therapy of leg ulcers and decubitus of ulcers with a xero-dressing: modern wound dressings with antibaterial activity. *H+G Brand* (Special Edition) **71**(9): 697–702

White RJ (2001) Managing exudate. *Nurs Times* **97**(9): 11–13

White RJ, Cooper R, Kingsley A (2001) Wound colonization and infection: the role of topical antimicrobials. *Br J Nurs* **10**(9): 563–78

Williams C (1994) Actisorb Plus in the treatment of exuding infected wounds. *Nurs Times* **3**(15): 786–8

Wunderlich U, Orfanos CE (1991) Behandlung der ulcera cruris venosa mit trockenen Wundauflagen. Phasenubergreifende Anwendung eines silber-impragnierten Aktivkohle-Xerodressings. *Hautarzt* **42**: 446–50

Zaki I, Shall L, Dalziel KL (1994) Bacitracin: a significant sensitizer in leg ulcer patients? *Contact Dermatitis* **31**: 92–4

# 11

# Changing wound-care practice: management of percutaneous endoscopic gastrostomy sites

*Kathy Leak*

Following the involvement of the wound-care service in the management of problem percutaneous endoscopic gastrostomy (PEG) sites in the Doncaster Trust, the scope of the service has been extended. In light of experience obtained from managing PEG sites and associated skin problems, and the evidence of clinical outcomes after treatment, educational and treatment policies have been implemented. These policies have raised the profile of the service and improved patient outcomes in the Trust and in areas of the community that have adopted our practices.

Too often nurses feel powerless; that their efforts do not influence or change practice (Castledine and McGee, 1998). However, by developing our practice and specializing in specific fields, nurses are becoming even more effective and efficient in care provision (Castledine, 2002). This efficiency provides the catalyst for change in practice. Articles focusing on nursing interventions that lead directly to improved patient outcomes highlight how circumstances can influence and change clinical practice, leading to the establishment of new nursing posts — and ultimately providing patients with a better quality of life.

Earlier this year, I published an article on work undertaken on skin problems after the insertion of percutaneous endoscopic gastrostomy (PEG) tubes (Leak, 2002). There was no specific follow-up care in the Trust for patients who had problems after the insertion of a PEG. Many patients lived in social isolation because of malodour and leakage from around the PEG tube (Leak, 2002). This isolation had a negative effect on their confidence and self-esteem, leading to further isolation. Owing to their intercurrent medical problems, such as stroke, many of these patients could not express their concern about their PEGs – or they did not want to complain because they were already dependent on their carers.

In May 2001, the wound-care service received a referral from a student nurse to see a patient with an irritated PEG site. The young man had severe multiple sclerosis and, consequently, difficulty communicating. On examination, the area surrounding his PEG was found to be overgranulating, macerated and very sore (*Figure 11.1*). The problem had gone on for a long time, and home carers had tried many products to protect the skin without success.

The wound-care nurse specialist's assessment of the PEG site identified overgranulation — and this was the ideal medium for bacterial colonization. Swab results showed 'normal skin flora', though this is probably a reflection of the failings of swabbing than a valid scientific finding (Beldon, 2001; Kingsley, 2001; Bowler, 2003).

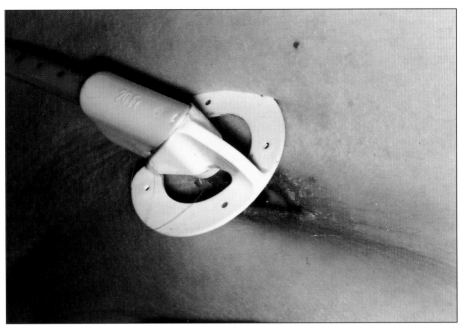

**Figure 11.1: Overgranulation of the PEG site**

The link between overgranulation (sometimes known as hypergranulation) and infection has been established, as has the fact that the associated exudate does not always indicate clinical infection (Young, 1995). However, in this case the increase in bacterial loading led to an increase in exudate, resulting in maceration to the surrounding skin.

Many courses of antibiotics had been used after reports by the nursing home staff of erythema around the PEG site. It became clear that this erythema was not the result of clinical infection, but of the maceration around the PEG site. Oral antibiotics gave only transitory relief by reducing the bacterial population around the PEG site. This case is a prime example of the misuse of antibiotics (Soulsbry, 1998) and such an approach cannot be regarded as appropriate first-line therapy. Such misuse gives rise to resistant strains of bacteria, such as methicillin-resistant *Staphylococcus aureus* (MRSA) in both hospitals and in the community (Cookson, 2000) and vancomycin-resistant enterococci (VRE; Centers for Disease Control and Prevention, 1995).

On careful assessment, it became clear that the overgranulation tissue was the main cause of the problem. The bacterial loading needed to be redressed and overgranulation tissue removed to prevent further maceration.

## A topical approach to management

Overuse of systemic antibiotics can be dangerous because of the risks of resistance, opportunistic infections and superinfection (Colsky *et al*, 1998; Soulsbry, 1998); they should be reserved for the treatment of spreading infection (Bowler *et al*, 2001). Topical antibiotics are of very limited value and should be reserved for specific, selected functions; they are not indicated for the routine treatment of colonized or infected wounds (*Drug and Therapeutics Bulletin*, 1991). However, topical antimicrobial agents are more useful. Those with a broad spectrum of action (eg. silver and iodine) have given rise to few reports of resistance. Topical preparations that provide sustained release of the active ingredient directly onto the lesion can also be used widely (*Chapter 3* [Cutting, 2001]; *Chapter 9* [White, 2001]). The latter feature is an advantage of antimicrobial dressings over solutions. To achieve a sufficient 'kill' of pathogens, the exposure to the active ingredient has to be of sufficient duration and concentration to be effective. Irrigation of wounds with antimicrobials is generally inappropriate: either the solution is too concentrated (and therefore toxic), or exposure is too short-lived to be effective.

### Silver

Silver has been used for many years and in different forms for problems with overgranulation tissue. Newer products include dressings impregnated with silver (*Chapter 3* [Cutting, 2001]; *Chapter 9* [White, 2001]). The silver is active against a wide range of organisms, including methicillin-resistant *Staphylococcus aureus* (Furr *et al*, 1994; *Chapter 12* [Jackson, 2001]). The antibacterial process *in vivo* is not visible to the eye and can take more than a week to manifest, so many carers do not always give the antibacterial product sufficient time to work (*Figure 11.2*).

When applied for long periods over large areas of skin or wound bed, silver-containing cream formulations may lead to absorption of silver into the systemic circulation. However, side-effects such as liver and kidney toxicity and skin staining (argyria) are rare (Marshall and Schneider, 1977; Lockhart *et al*, 1983; Kulick *et al*, 1985; Fung and Bowen, 1996). There are no reports of these effects from any silver-containing wound dressing.

Through our own practice, we have found that Actisorb Silver 220 dressing (Johnson and Johnson) is the safest and most effective approach to managing PEG-site infections. This product includes a broad-spectrum antimicrobial and does not donate appreciable quantities of silver to the wound bed. The inclusion of an activated charcoal fabric reduces odour and helps the absorption of bacterial endotoxins (Millward, 1991; Müller *et al*, 2003). The cost might initially appear high because the dressing may need changing daily, but when exudate levels decrease, the product can be left *in situ* for longer periods (*Figure 11.3*).

**Figure 11.2: Colonized PEG site**

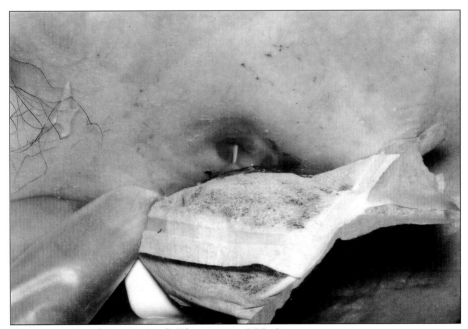

**Figure 11.3: Applying Actisorb Silver 220 to PEG site**

Actisorb Silver 220 dressing has been used successfully on a large number of patients in our trust, resulting in a reduction or removal of overgranulation tissue; this, in turn, leads to a fall in exudate levels and an improvement in the surrounding maceration over a one-week period (Leak, 2002).

In early 2000, ward rounds in the Doncaster Royal Infirmary identified eight inpatients with PEG problems in the 1500-bed hospital; all the PEGs were overgranulated and leaking. A consultation was sought with endoscopy staff, who acknowledged that there was a problem within the community for follow-up patients with these difficulties — and no effective treatment protocols. Consequently, problems with PEG sites in patients in the community were not identified early enough or were managed inappropriately, both leading to the need for hospitalization.

By providing clinic and home visit time, we were able to make a 'preventative effort'. In the sixteen-month period from May 2001 to September 2002, we saw 204 patients — an average of thirteen patients per month.

Numbers of referrals to the wound-care service are steadily increasing as word spreads; as a result, we have seen some very bad cases. One lady in her seventies presented with maceration from her nipples to her groin with what looked like a yeast growth that was later confirmed by swab results. Actisorb Silver 220 was applied and changed daily for one week, then on alternate days. The area completely healed within three weeks. The patient revealed that she had been in this condition for six months, changing her clothes several times a day.

We also discovered that she did not like to sit still for long periods and forced her nutritional requirements of two litres down the PEG tube within ten minutes, rather than overnight, causing it to leak through the insertion site onto the skin, leading to yeast growth.

Another patient presented in casualty with a leaking tube. Inexperienced medical staff decided it was not the tube that was causing the problem and admitted the patient to a ward.

The patient was seen by staff from wound care and endoscopy. The site was excoriated (*Figure 11.4*) and silver dressings prescribed. The tube needed to be changed because water was seen seeping from the base. Unfortunately, medical staff decided a change was not necessary and discharged the patient back to the nursing home (he is in long-term care for multiple sclerosis).

Two days later the patient arrived in casualty again. The site had deteriorated and the tube was still leaking (*Figure 11.5*). This time, endoscopy and wound-care personnel located the medical staff responsible and the tube was eventually changed. Actisorb Silver 220 was applied to the site with excellent outcome after only one week (*Figure 11.6*). The nursing staff, patient and relatives were happy with the eventual outcome.

Incidents such as this have led to the establishment of the post of PEG nurse in the endoscopy department. The post provides a specialist nursing service for patients with PEG problems. A clinic has been set up to provide wound care and home visits. The nurse carries out routine changes of PEG 'buttons' and other necessary procedures that have traditionally been done by the medical team, thereby freeing up consultant time and increasing the expertise of nurses.

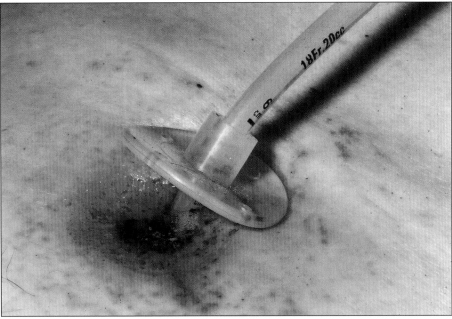

**Figure 11.4: Leaking from overgranulated PEG site**

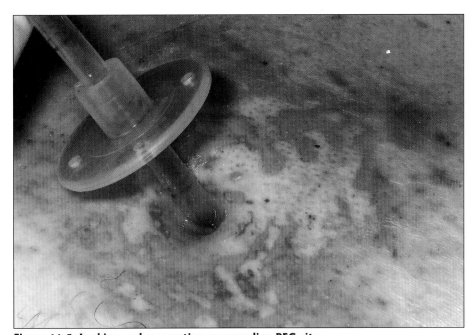

**Figure 11.5: Leaking and maceration surrounding PEG site**

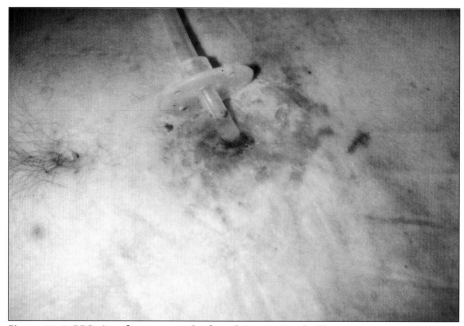

**Figure 11.6: PEG site after one week of applying Actisorb Silver 220**

This new service is used by many patients; numbers have increased dramatically. A record is kept of each patient and overall numbers of consultations recorded. Now the service is running, research can be done to verify that the work is effective and efficient. As a result of research and implementation of a change in practice there has been a 50% reduction in hospital admissions due to PEG site problems. Most patients are now adequately cared for in the community with the input of the hospital PEG nurse. The use of Actisorb Silver 220 on PEG sites has resulted in a substantial reduction in MRSA isolates from PEG sites.

Silver dressings have an important role to play in wound care, present and future. Although reports in medical journals testify to their safety and efficacy (White *et al*, 2001), there is a reluctance to use silver dressings — perhaps because they do not yield results overnight. Silver-containing dressings do have a place in problem PEG site management.

## Key points

❖ Our continuing work on PEG sites has identified a need for a clinical nurse specialist.

❖ Further experience with the charcoal-containing silver dressing confirms our positive impression of the clinical value of this product.

❖ Where PEG problems arise, it is important to avoid the inappropriate use of systemic or topical antibiotics, and to treat in the most clinically effective fashion.

# References

Beldon P (2001) How to diagnose infection. *Institute of Wound Management News* **4**(1): 3–5

Bowler PG (2003) The 10(5) bacterial growth guideline: reassessing its clinical relevance in wound healing. *Ostomy, Wound Management* **49**(1): 44–53

Bowler PG, Duerden BI, Armstrong DG (2001) Wound microbiology and associated approaches to wound management. *Clin Microbiol Rev* **14**: 244–69

Castledine G, McGee P, eds (1998) *Advanced and Specialist Nursing Practice.* Blackwell Scientific, Oxford

Castledine G (2002) The important aspects of nurse specialist roles. *Br J Nurs* **11**(5): 350

Colsky AS, Kisner R, Kerdel F (1998) Analysis of antibiotic susceptibilities of skin flora in hospitalized dermatology patients. The crisis of antibiotic resistance has come to the surface. *Arch Dermatol* **134**: 1006–9

Cookson BD (2000) Methicillin-resistant *Staphylococcus aureus* in the community: new battlefronts, or are the battles lost? *Infect Control Hosp Epidemiol* **21**(6): 398–403

Cutting KF (2001) A dedicated follower of fashion? Topical medications and wounds. *Br J Nurs* **10** (Silver Supplement): 9–18

Centers for Disease Control and Prevention (1995) Recommendations for preventing the spread of vancomycin resistance. Recommendations of the Hospital Control Practices Advisory Committee (HICPAC). *MMWR* **44**(rr-12): 1–13

Drug and Therapeutics Bulletin (1991) Local applications to wounds 1: cleansers, antibacterials, debriders. *Drug Ther Bull* **29**(24): 93–5

Fung MC, Bowen DL (1996) Silver products for medical indications: risk-benefit assessment. *Clin Toxicol* **34**(1): 119–26

Furr JR, Russell AD, Turner TD, Andrews A (1994) Antibacterial activity of ACTISORB* PLUS, ACTISORB* and silver nitrate. *J Hosp Infect* **22**: 201–8

Jackson L (2001) Use of a charcoal dressing silver on an MRSA-infected wound. *Br J Community Nurs* **7**(12 Silver Supplement 2): 19–26

Kingsley A (2001) A proactive approach to wound infection. *Nurs Standard* **15**(30): 50–8

Kulick MI, Wong R, Okarma TB *et al* (1985) Prospective study of side-effects associated with the use of silver sulfadiazine in severely burned patients. *Ann Plast Surg* **14**(5): 407–18

Leak K (2002) PEG site infections: a novel use for Actisorb Silver 220. *Br J Community Nurs* **7**(6): 321–5

Lockhart SP, Rushworth A, Azmy AAF, Raine PAM (1983) Topical silver sulphadiazine: side-effects and urinary excretion. *Burns* **10**(9): 9–12

Marshall JP, Schneider RP (1977) Systemic argyria secondary to topical silver nitrate. *Arch Dermatol* **113**: 1077–8

Millward P (1991) Comparing treatment for leg ulcers. *Nurs Times* **87**(13): 70–2

Müller G, Winkler Y, Kramer A (2003) Antibacterial activity and endotoxin binding capacity of Actisorb Silver 220. *J Hosp Infect* **53**(3): 211–14

Soulsbry (1998) *Resistance to antibiotics and other antimicrobial agents. House of Lords Select Committee for Science and Technology, 7th report.* HMSO, London

White RJ (2001) A charcoal dressing with silver in wound infection: clinical evidence. *Br J Nurs* (Silver Supplement 2): 4–8

Young T (1995) Common problems in wound care: overgranulation. *Br J Nurs* **4**(3): 169–70

# 12

# Use of a charcoal dressing with silver on an MRSA-infected wound

*Lorraine Jackson*

This chapter explores the rationale for the dressing selection in the treatment of a methicillin-resistant *Staphylococcus aureus* (MRSA) surgical wound infection. It looks at the evidence to support the selection of the dressing for the actions it performs in reducing infection. It considers the implications of the immunosuppressed patient and the necessity to remove the risk of MRSA from both a medical and a quality of life issue, as infection to a dialysis access point in an already compromised person is a serious problem. The cost implications and the dilemma that is faced when treating an MRSA infection are discussed, giving consideration to the potential resistance issues. Bacteria are known to impair the repair process and as they proliferate in the wound each process involved in healing is affected, it is only when this equilibrium is in balance that the normal process of wound healing can occur. Therefore, the dressing selection process involves those dressings with the ability to reduce bacterial colonization and restore the wound balance.

Infected wounds are not only costly to the patient — resulting in distress, pain and delayed healing — but are a financial drain on health services through increased length of hospital stay (Leigh, 1981) and increased treatment costs. In particular, hospital-acquired infections (HAIs) are a substantial burden to the health service, tax-payers, and to the patient. The period of hospitalisation is usually increased, patients often require more antibiotics and analgesia, and more dressings and nursing time, whether they are in hospital or have returned to the community.

According to recent data, infections of surgical wounds are among the most common hospital-acquired infections (Public Health Laboratory Service [PHLS], 2000). It has been estimated that each patient with a surgical site infection requires an additional hospital stay of 6.5 days, and hospital costs are doubled (Plowman *et al*, 2000). In a recent survey, 47% of the microorganisms identified as causing infections at surgical sites in English hospitals were staphylococci; 81% were *Staphylococcus aureus*, of which 61% were methicillin-resistant (MRSA) (PHLS, 2000).

Community MRSA (defined as isolates from GP and other community-submitted specimens) is an increasing problem in nursing and residential homes, and among patients discharged from hospital with MRSA who spread it to non-hospitalised patients (Cookson, 2000). As an emerging problem, the control of community MRSA requires careful consideration of all available preventive and control measures.

*Staphylococcus aureus* is a Gram-positive aerobic bacterium that produces the enzyme coagulase. It is carried in the nose, throat, axillae, toe webs and perineum of 30–50% of healthy people without causing clinical infection. Asymptomatic carriage is clinically significant because the bacteria can be transferred to susceptible sites or from a fit asymptomatic individual to someone less healthy who will succumb to clinical infection. *Staphylococcus aureus* in general is considered to be the single most problematic bacterium in traumatic, surgical and burn wound infections (Mertz *et al*, 1999; Bowler *et al*, 2001). MRSA causes a wide spectrum of infections (Hill, 1993).

The treatment of choice for MRSA infections is systemic vancomycin. Topical treatment of MRSA-infected wounds has met with variable results. The topical antibiotic mupirocin has been used successfully, however, long-term intermittent use has led to resistance in many cases (Irish, 1998). Silver has been found to be effective topically against both MRSA and vancomycin-resistant enterococci (VRE) (Silver, 1991; Schworth, 1995; Yoshida *et al*, 1997; Rudolph *et al*, 2000).

| Table 12.1: Advantages of the topical approach to methicillin-resistant *Staphylococcus aureus* control using silver (or other antiseptic agents) |
| --- |
| Immediately available for antibacterial action: not reliant on the blood system for bioavailability |
| Silver has not yet been found to select for resistance |
| Topical dressing therapy is safe, effective and economical for hospital and community use |

The topical approach to MRSA control using silver (or some other antiseptic agents) does have advantages, whether as a monotherapy or in combination with systemic antibiotics. These are outlined in *Table 12.1*.

It is important to remember that the presence of bacteria does not necessarily mean that the wound is infected, as two patients may react differently to the same number or type of bacteria. What is important is the individual's response — the host reaction to the pathogen in the wound (Ayliffe *et al*, 1992). Gilchrist (1997) differentiated the bacterial burden:

- contamination is the presence of bacteria without multiplication
- colonization occurs when there is multiplication, but no host reaction
- infection is deposition and multiplication of bacteria in tissue with an associated host reaction.

Any immunosuppressive condition or medication, or other factor known to compromise healing, will influence the patient's ability to respond to the infective organism. The categories of wound colonization, critical colonization and infection have been recently defined further (Kingsley, 2001).

The phagocytic action of neutrophils and macrophages helps protect injured tissue from infection, however, patients with systemic conditions such as uncontrolled diabetes, systemic steroid therapy, poor vascularization or immune incompetence are at greater risk of infection because of their diminished defences (Dow *et al*, 1999). Bacteria impair repair processes by producing toxic by-products and competing with body cells for oxygen and nutrients (Robson *et al*, 1990).

As bacteria proliferate in the wound, each process involved in healing is affected. It is only when this equilibrium is in balance that the normal process of wound healing can occur (Robson, 1988). This must be in conjunction with addressing the systemic factors that influence wound healing.

## Patient history

'Tony' is a twenty-eight-year-old male who has insulin dependent diabetes mellitus (IDDM – type 1) and is in end-stage renal failure secondary to diabetic nephropathy. As a result of diabetic retinopathy, he is now registered blind. His past medical history is complex, having had failed continuous ambulatory peritoneal dialysis (CAPD), hypertension and vascular access problems. He has had two previous failed renal transplants, and currently receives haemodialysis three times per week.

The transplant registrar made a referral to the tissue viability service on 6 August 1999 for wound care advice and management. 'Tony' had undergone a graft nephrectomy on 27 July resulting in a large wound in the left iliac fossa. After the failed kidney had been removed, the wound exposed two fluid collections, superior and inferior to where the kidney had been situated, and an abdominal wall abscess. The resultant wound was left open, forming a cavity to the level of the deep tension sutures.

Until the tissue viability service were called in the surgical team had managed the postoperative wound care. Care entailed twice-daily 'packing' of the cavity using povidone-iodine soaked gauze, causing considerable pain during the procedure (Thomas, 1989). The packing also caused notable discomfort when *in situ*, enough to cause 'Tony' positional discomfort and sleep disturbance.

As a result, subcutaneous morphine was required before dressing changes and a gaseous mixture of 50% oxygen and 50% nitrous oxide (Entonox®, BOC Gases, Manchester) was administered during the dressing change. A slow release morphine analgesic regime was implemented to control generalised pain.

By 2 August, the transplant surgical team had conducted further surgical debridement of the wound. A hydrogen peroxide and a povidone-iodine washout were performed in theatre. The surgical team felt this appropriate to deal with the slough at the wound bed and infection of the wound. The wound had been confirmed MRSA positive as a result of tissue samples taken during previous surgery.

The definition of a surgical wound infection is that the wound contains more than $10^6$ bacteria per gram of tissue (Robson and Heggers, 1984). However, it is important to remember that a clinical infection can develop in the presence of fewer microorganisms if the host immune response is compromised and if the bacterial bioburden becomes greater than $10^5$–$10^6$ per gram of tissue or millilitre of exudates (Cutting, 1998; Robson, 1999; Miller, 2001).

The complex nature of 'Tony's' medical history indicated that his wound would be a major challenge to heal. Furthermore, he was being treated with an immunosuppressive drug (cyclosporin) to reduce the risk of graft rejection. Cyclosporin inhibits immune rejection of the transplanted kidney; unfortunately, it can affect the immune response to all antigens as well, so compromising the typical inflammatory response. The patient's body may therefore fail to activate the normal healing process (Cutting, 1994).

Nutrition is also an issue with the renal patient, as high levels of protein are excreted from diseased kidneys. The high exudate loss from infected wounds further exacerbates protein loss; Breslow (1991) discussed the effect on nutritional status as a loss of 90–100g of protein per day in exudates from a cavity pressure ulcer. Therefore, there is a high potential for malnutrition in this group of compromised patients.

However, for most patients with renal disease protein intake levels are kept to a minimum, 1–1.2g per kilo of body weight. This supply is drained by the catabolic demand on the body by haemodialysis. Depletion in protein levels will lead to delayed collagen synthesis, and interruption of granulation tissue formation (McLaren, 1992) so affecting the quality and speed of healing. In diabetes mellitus the balance between metabolic demand and energy intake is altered as the disease affects the utilisation of carbohydrates for energy needs within the cell; this impairs healing rates (Fahey *et al*, 1991).

## Treatment

When the tissue viability nurse (TVN) initially inspected the wound on 6 August the cavity walls were relatively clean — although traumatised from the gauze removal — but the wound bed had a covering of thick slough and was readily draining pus. Suppuration is the result of liquefaction of tissues in the presence of microorganisms, indicating wound infection.

The TVN advised cleansing the wound bed initially using pressurised irrigation with warmed saline. This removed loose debris and slough without causing trauma, and aimed to provide an optimum healing environment by also removing some of the conditions for the multiplication of bacteria. High pressure irrigation has been shown to lower the infection rates in contaminated wounds (Chisholm, 1992).

Silicone-coated knitted viscose dressing (N-A Ultra, Johnson & Johnson Medical Ltd, Ascot) was used to line the cavity to reduce any potential adherence (Thomas, 1994). Adherence of the dressing to a wound can exacerbate infection; Lawrence *et al* (1992) found that dry dressings, such as gauze, stick to the wound and their removal has been demonstrated to spread bacteria by aerosol formation.

The cavity was then gently and loosely packed with an activated charcoal dressing with silver (Actisorb Silver 220, Johnson & Johnson Medical Ltd, Ascot). The silver imparts antimicrobial properties (Russell and Hugo, 1994) and these were desirable with this particular wound due to the MRSA infection. White *et al* (2001) discussed that measures should be taken to reduce the level of causative organisms especially with an organ transplant patient threatened with MRSA.

In such a situation the surgical wound is at risk, especially as the immuno-suppressed status of the patient increases the possibility of life-threatening infection. The charcoal in Actisorb Silver 220 adsorbs bacteria and their spores, which become attached to the charcoal filaments (Coombs, 1981) containing them within the dressing structure for the antibacterial silver to act. Silver is known to produce structural changes within bacterial cells (Russell and Hugo, 1994), leading to bacterial death.

The primary dressings were secured using a semipermeable film dressing to allow observation of the peri-wound margin. The ward nursing staff, in conjunction with the transplant surgical team, commenced daily dressing changes. This initial dressing change was completed with the existing analgesic regime in order to remove the gauze packing used by the transplant surgical team. Following the initial change, Entonox® was the only analgesia required for dressing changes during the first forty-eight hours. Thereafter, no analgesia was needed during dressing changes.

The wound was reviewed after four days on 10 August and photographed (*Figure 12.1*). At this dressing change no trauma was noted to the cavity walls, although the wound bed was still discharging copious amounts of pus. The colour, amount and composition of exudate can provide valuable information to identify the stage of healing of the wound, any presence of infection and underlying tracts or fistulae (Nelson, 1997). This was a concern with this wound as its origin was the two collections surrounding the failed kidney.

Over subsequent dressing changes the wear time of the dressing increased to three- to four-day intervals. Steady progress was noted; the pus levels reduced, reflecting a reduction in the bacterial bioburden. As the infection level decreased, the wound was able to progress from the inflammatory phase.

Wound swabs (taken as per hospital protocol as part of the screening process for MRSA linked to the treatment policy of the trust) were reported as negative on 20 August — two weeks after commencing use of Actisorb Silver 220 — and remained negative on subsequent swabs. Swabs from other sites on 'Tony's' body eventually returned negative and following three consecutive multi-site negatives 'Tony' was declared free of MRSA. A further photograph taken 27 August (seventeen days after commencing the Actisorb Silver 220 regime) (*Figure 12.2*) showed a completely clean granulating wound with some evidence of epithelialization on the margin.

'Tony's' wound continued to progress well, and he was discharged home in mid-September with the haemodialysis nursing team caring for the wound on dialysis visits, and general supervision by the district nurses. This provided the opportunity to follow 'Tony's' care through to the final stages of wound healing. Exudate levels continued to decrease over this period and the wound progressed through the proliferative phase of healing to the point where the dressing regime was changed on 21 September, forty-six days after starting use of Actisorb Silver 220.

The end result was complete wound healing by mid-November (*Figure 12.3*). The wound was photographed 19 November, 110 days after the surgeon's initial referral.

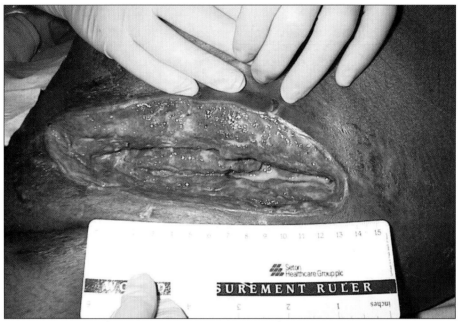

**Figure 12.1: Wound on 10 August. Note quantity of pus**

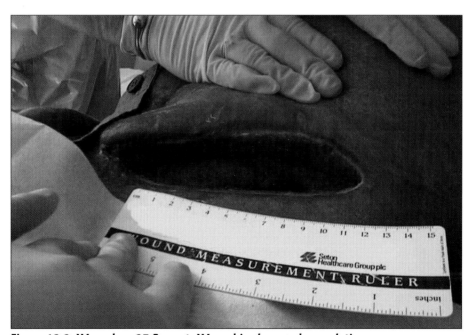

**Figure 12.2: Wound on 27 August. Wound is clean and granulating**

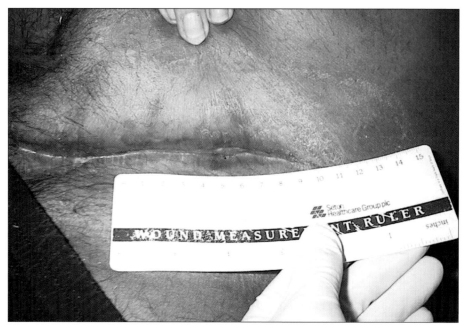

**Figure 12.3: Wound on 19 November. Note complete closure**

## Discussion

The eradication of the MRSA infection was the main priority to facilitate wound healing in this compromised patient. Treatment was primarily directed towards the removal of the infection in order to optimize healing potential, especially in light of the complex medical history and influencing systemic factors.

Actisorb Silver 220 proved an effective dressing due to its ability to reduce bacterial colonization. The removal of the risk of MRSA from 'Tony' was both a medical and a quality of life issue, as infection to a dialysis access point in an already compromised person is a serious medical problem.

The dressing's ability to remain effective in the presence of exudate facilitated rapid cleaning of the wound and eradication of the MRSA. This also reflected on 'Tony's' quality of life, as exudate levels were managed, preventing peri-wound maceration, and any odour from the resultant infection was controlled by the carbon cloth adsorbing small gas and liquid 'malodour' molecules.

For anyone, let alone such a young person, wound odour can soon socially isolate them from friends, and if frequent dressing changes are needed it can be very restrictive to their activities; free time is precious when one has to attend dialysis three times per week.

'Tony' was involved in decisions regarding his wound care — he was enthusiastic to do so. Clinical governance promotes working in partnership with patients, offering them the choice to decide what their needs are through empowerment. Ritualised practice engenders a culture of control over the patient

— who is viewed as a passive recipient of care — and is no longer acceptable (Watret and White, 2001).

'Tony' found this dressing regime comfortable, reducing his requirements for strong analgesia. The ability to move once a dressing was applied and return to a more independent life was important to 'Tony' (the results of an independent interview with 'Tony' are shown in *Figure 12.4*. The interview was conducted in October 2001).

The Royal College of Surgeons report on postoperative pain (1990) stated that it is a moral imperative to relieve pain and patients should not have to suffer pain. This certainly applies to wound pain.

In 'Tony's' case, reduction in the need for pain management led to a reduction in nursing time required, as qualified staff were no longer needed to administer the Entonox®. The dressing frequency diminished, saving nursing time, and saving money.

Implementation of this dressing regime allowed the wound to pass through the normal stages of wound healing without the compromise of infection. This was a very important factor considering the healing process was already compromised by diabetes mellitus, nutrition and immune status. To achieve such rapid results is a tribute to the whole multi-disciplinary hospital and community team involved in 'Tony's' care.

## Key points

❖ Silver has been found to be effective topically against both MRSA and vancomycin-resistant enterococci (VRE).

❖ The silver in Actisorb Silver 220 is immediately available for anti-bacterial action in the wound and not reliant on the blood system for bioavailability, and silver has not yet been found to select for resistance.

❖ Antimicrobial therapy using medicated dressings is safe and effective for both hospital and community use.

❖ Actisorb Silver 220 proved a comfortable and effective dressing in the case study due to its non-adherence and ability to reduce bacterial colonization. The ability of the dressing to remain effective in the presence of exudate facilitated rapid cleaning of the wound and eradication of the MRSA.

❖ Quality of life improvement was achieved as exudate levels were managed, preventing peri-wound maceration, dressing changes were pain-free, and malodour controlled. Improved comfort reduced analgesic requirements and returned the patient to a more independent life.

❖ Nursing time was reduced as the need for pain management was reduced and the dressing change frequency diminished. Fewer dressing changes had a cost effective benefit.

---

**Q.** What were your concerns about your nephrectomy wound?

**A.** My initial concern was the weeping… It got to a point where the dressing was put on and within 4/6 hours the wound would be wet and I would have to call the surgeon again to come and change it. Obviously I had to get up and sit up, it was the general pain on movement and the weeping. My concern after the nephrectomy was what they had found after they'd taken the kidney out, what was behind it ['Tony' is referring to abscesses]. The weeping got so bad after about three weeks after they'd taken the kidney out they had to take me down to theatre to clear it out. Then after they'd cleared it out they called [the TVN] in and she had a look at it and put Actisorb Silver in…to see how it goes. It was just like trial and error really, just to see if this could help it in any way.

**Q.** Did you have any fears or concerns, in particular when you found out that the wound was MRSA positive?

**A.** No because I had MRSA before that. I was infected with MRSA before that when I had a line in my neck for my kidney dialysis. I caught MRSA from there because it was on the ward. So when I went in there to have my line put in my leg and my neck after my fistula failed for my kidney dialysis when I had to have a line put in. It was only then when I had it put in and after that I got MRSA and that's when I started getting abscess problems trying to get the access to get to my blood. That's when they knew the MRSA was there and all the time the MRSA was just following me around. I couldn't shrug it off. The kidney had already failed and all of a sudden I started getting pains in the kidney and they took some scans and they could see something like water coming from behind it… they didn't know what was behind it, and they drained that out a couple of times and it was only then that they saw what was behind it. It was infection. MRSA. All they could do was pack it. The surgeon couldn't close it up and he could get his actual hand, his whole hand, into the wound up to his wrist. That's how deep the wound was.

**Q.** Did you have any particular experience of pain with the original wound treatment?

**A.** Yes! I was on Entonox gas and drugs for the wound packing because it involved an uncomfortable pushing-in motion. It was… just packing in an empty hole. That's what they had to do. With gauze they were hopeful that it would soak it all up and draw it all out. As they found later on the gauze wasn't doing anything. It was just soaking up some of the stuff that was there but the pain was always there, it just wouldn't stop.

**Q.** What sort of pain did you have?

**A.** It was an uncomfortable sort of a numbness really... every time I moved or sat up it would hurt. When I lay down it would hurt. It was just everywhere, with me all the time. They tried me on different pain killers but these would just stop it for a little while. It was just the fact that if I sat in one position and stayed there it was alright, but when I started moving... but I thought I can't sit still all day and I can't lie still all day. That's where the pain was.

**Q.** So how did you feel when you were referred to the tissue viability nurse?

**A.** I'd never met [the TVN] before... when she came to see me she looked at the situation and saw what they were doing to it and asked them everything about what they were putting in it. [She] initially did start with Actisorb Silver.

**Q.** Did you have any concerns or reservations about the recommended treatment?

**A.** No, none at all. If it was going to help me then I accepted it. She just told me basically it looks like a teabag ['Tony' is blind] and works with a trap effect. It would soak up what infection was in there. It would pull it all out. You know I felt the gauze... they were all, soaking. It was basically just sitting in there all soaked. The first time they took the Actisorb out it was wet, quite wet. But, it drew all infection out and then the minute that it was in I felt comfortable. When it was in the wound it felt comfortable and I could lie down a bit better.

**Q.** The pain was less?

**A.** The pain was less. Things were sort of going in the right direction the minute that went in. They had put the Actisorb [Silver 220] in, it was different. Straight away I could notice the difference. It was pulling it all out, the infection, you know, taking all the rubbish out basically. It was drawing all the infection out and then the pain got less. Instead of the surgeon coming to see me in the morning and then late evening, about a week after the Actisorb Silver had gone in, he felt that he only needed to come once a day. I asked him why, he said well whatever [the TVN has] put in there has drawn the infection.

**Q.** Did you feel like it was combating the infection as well?

**A.** Yes, straight away. Straight away I knew... It was drawing it all out, all the infection was coming out. And then I think it wasn't until the later stage, about two months after we'd had the Actisorb in there, that they did the screening. They screened me again for MRSA I had three swabs taken. The first one that came back positive and then they waited a week and then the other two came back negative. And they couldn't work it out why it had come back negative. They thought there must be something wrong. So I went on another couple of weeks with the Actisorb Silver and the wound was getting smaller by itself, it was starting to close in and the surgeon couldn't believe it. They screened me again, all three came back negative. I said, 'What does that mean?'. And they said, 'Well the MRSA has gone, out of the wound'. They carried on with the Actisorb Silver and then it just kept closing and then eventually the surgeon himself was going. He'd got a job somewhere else.

So then it got to a point where he was coming in and he was telling the nurses to come and watch him do the dressing, to pack it with this Actisorb Silver. So that when he eventually left and put it in the nurses' hands… Eventually the wound got smaller and smaller and they said I could go home.

**Q.** How long did that take?

**A.** Three months. From when I first had the nephrectomy up to the end of July, those first three or four weeks, it was packing with gauze and we weren't really getting anywhere, going in and out of theatre, made two trips to the theatre to have it cleaned out, under sterile conditions. They used those vacuum things, they put me under general anaesthetic and had a good clean out… and they could get their hand in and give it a good clean out, but while I was on the ward he couldn't really do much with it.

**Q.** Would you say that you were confident with the treatment you received there?

**A.** Yeah, very good. Especially after the Actisorb Silver went in. I was alright with that.

**Q.** So, in summary…

**A.** I think with some of the nurses it's trial and error. I found when I had the wound on my leg, and my nephrectomy it got to a point when they thought 'well our way isn't working so we've got to ask somebody else' and that's when they called [the TVN] in. But I thought what would have happened if they said our way was the best, you know if they'd carried on with gauze packing. I wonder if the wound would ever close up. The fact that they were saying our way's the best, the nurses were. Until [the TVN] came on the scene and she looked at it and she had a different solution. I don't think that [she] was happy with the way they were dressing it. Once I had Actisorb Silver in, the surgeon would come in the morning before his theatre list, and then at night when his list had finished — he was doing this twice a day for three or four weeks.

**Q.** Finally, what would you say that the benefit of using Actisorb has been for you?

**A.** It's benefited me loads… It drew out all my MRSA and I never got MRSA again. I have never had it to this day. Its been two years now. I can't fail it at all. Every time I get a new wound that's the first thing that I tell them. When I had my amputation this year, they did it again!

They didn't know what to do with it. I said 'call [the TVN], she'll know'. 'Sorry, but she doesn't work here' they replied and then I was lost. When they rang the other nurse, the TVN at [Leicester Royal Infirmary], she was the one who told them over the 'phone. She didn't come here and actually look at the wound. And when she said to put Actisorb Silver in I knew straight away, I was at peace then, I knew straight away that something was going to happen to this wound. And it did. And it cleared it up. That's all I can say.

**Figure 12.4: Independent interview with 'Tony' conducted on 4 October 2001**

# References

Ayliffe GA, Lowbury EJ, Gebbes AM (1992) *Control of Hospital Infection*. Chapman & Hall, London

Bowler PG, Duerden BI, Armstrong DG (2001) Wound microbiology and associated approaches to wound management. *Clin Micro Rev* **14**(2): 244–69

Breslow R (1991) Nutrition status and dietary intake of patients with pressure ulcers: review of research literature 1943–1989. *Decubitus* **4**(1): 16–21

Chisholm C (1992) Wound evaluation and cleansing. *Emerg Med Clin North Am* **10**(4): 665–72

Cookson BD (2000) Methicillin-resistant *Staphylococcus aureus* in the community: new battlefronts, or are the battles lost? *Infect Control Hosp Epidemiol* **21**(6) 398–403

Coombs TJ (1981) More than a wound dressing. *Health Soc Serv J* **91**(4768): 1268–9

Cutting KF (1994) Detecting infection. *Nurs Times* **90**(50): 60–2

Cutting KF (1998) *Wounds and Infection*. Wound Care Society, London: 2

Davey P, Hernanz C, Lynch W *et al* (1991) Human and non-financial costs of hospital acquired infection. *J Hosp Infect* (supplement) **18**: 79-84

Dow G, Browne A, Sibbald G (1999) Infection in chronic wounds: controversies in diagnosis and treatment. *Ostomy, Wound Management* **45**: 31

Fahey TJ, Sadaty A, Jones WG *et al* (1991) Diabetes impairs the inflammatory response to wound healing. *J Surg Res* **50**: 308–13

Gilchrist B (1997) Infection and culturing. In: Krasner D, Kanes D, eds. *Chronic Wound Care: A Clinical Source Book for Health Care Professionals*. 2nd edn. Health Management Publications, Wayne, PA: 109–15

Hill RL, Duckworth GJ, Casewell MW (1993) Elimination of nasal carriage of methicillin-resistant *Staphylococcus aureus* with mupirocin during a hospital outbreak. *J Antimicrob Chemother* **22**(3): 377–84

Irish D, Eltringham I, Teall A, Pickett H, Farelly H, Reith S, Woodford N, Cookson B (1998) Control of an outbreak of an epidemic methicillin-resistant *Staphylococcus aureus* also resistant to mupirocin. *J Hosp Infect* **39**(11): 19–26

Kingsley A (2001) A proactive approach to wound infection. *Nurs Standard* **15**(30): 50–8

Lawrence JC, Lilly HA, Kidson A (1992) Wound dressings and airborne dispersal of bacteria. *Lancet* **339**: 807

Leigh DA (1981) An eight-year study of postoperative wound infection in two district general hospitals. *J Hosp Infect* **2**: 207–17

McLaren SMG (1992) Nutrition and wound healing. *J Wound Care* **1**(3): 45–55

Mertz PM, Oliveira-Gandia MF, Davis S (1999) The evaluation of cadexomer iodine wound dressing on methicillin resistant *Staphylococcus aureus* (MRSA) in acute wounds. *Dermatol Surg* **25**(2): 89–93

Miller M (2001) Wound infection unravelled. *J Community Nurs* **15**(3): 31–6

Nelson EA (1997) Is exudates a clinical problem? A nurse's perspective. In: Cherry G, Harding KG, eds. *Management of Wound Exudate*. SOFOS, Oxford

Plowman R, Graves N, Griffen M *et al* (2000) *The Socio-economic Burden of Hospital Acquired Infection*. Public Health Laboratory Service, London

Public Health Laboratory Service (2000) *Surveillance of Surgical Site Infection in English Hospitals data 1997–1999*. Public Health Laboratory Service, London

Robson MC, Heggers JP (1984) Quantitative bacteriology and inflammatory mediators in soft tissue. In: Hunt T, Heppenstall R, Pines E, Rovee D, eds. *Soft and Hard Tissue Repair*. Praegar Publications, New York

Robson MC (1988) Disturbances in wound healing. *Ann Emerg Med* **17**: 1274–78

Robson MC, Stenberg BD, Heggers JP (1990) Wound healing alterations caused by infection. *Clin Plast Surg* **17**: 485–90

Robson MC (1999) Lessons gleaned from the sport of wound watching. *Wound Repair Regen* **7**(1): 2–6

Royal College of Surgeons (1990) *Commission on the Provision of Surgical Services: Report of the Working Party on Pain after Surgery*. Royal College of Surgeons, London

Rudolph P, Werner H-P, Kramer A (2000) Studies on the microbiocidal efficacy of wound dressings (Untersuchungen zur Mikrobizidie von Wundauflagen). *Hygiene & Medezin* **5**(25): 184–6

Russell AD, Hugo WB (1994) Antimicrobial activity and action of silver. *Prog Med Chem* **31**: 351–70

Schworth D (1995) *Actisorb Plus: Test of Efficiency Against a Multi-resistant S. aureus (MRSA)*. Austrian Institute for Biomedical Materials Engineering, Vienna

Silver HJ (1991) MRSA in long-term skilled nursing facilities. *Infect Control Hosp Epidemiol* **12**(2): 76–8

Thomas S (1989) Pain and wound management. *Community Outlook* 12 July: 11–15

Thomas S (1994) Low-adherence dressings. *J Wound Care* **3**(1): 27-30

Watret L, White RJ (2001) Surgical wound management: the role of dressings. *Nurs Standard* **15**(44): 59–69

White RJ, Cooper R, Kingsley A (2001) Wound colonization and infection: the role of topical antimicrobials. *Br J Nurs* **10**(9): 563–78

Yoshida T, Ohura T, Sugihara T *et al* (1997) Clinical efficacy of silver sulphadiazine for ulcerative skin lesions infected with MRSA. *J Antibiot* (Tokyo) **50**(1): 39–44